CATLORE

CATLORE

Desmond Morris

JONATHAN CAPE
THIRTY-TWO BEDFORD SQUARE LONDON

First published 1987
Copyright © 1987 by Desmond Morris

Jonathan Cape Ltd, 32 Bedford Square, London WC1B 3EL

British Library Cataloguing in Publication Data

Morris, Desmond
Catlore.
1. Cats – Behaviour
I. Title
636.8   SF446.5

ISBN 0-224-02520-1

Typeset by Computape (Pickering) Ltd, North Yorkshire
Printed in Great Britain by
The Alden Press Ltd, Oxford

Contents

Introduction

For thousands of years the domestic cat has aroused strong emotions in its human companions. In ancient Egypt it was adored to the point of worship, and cat-killing was punishable by death. In the Dark Ages of Europe the mood changed dramatically and the cat was savagely persecuted by the Christian Church. For centuries its association with witchcraft and black magic gave it an air of mystery and caused it to suffer endless torment at the hands of the pious. It was the sentimentality of the Victorians in the nineteenth century that finally rescued it and restored it to the role of a loved household pet. Since then, in modern times, its popularity has risen steadily. Today there are about six million cats in Britain. Of these five million are well cared for as companion animals in the home. One million are strays, managing somehow to survive in country fields and city alleyways.

Everywhere the cat numbers are multiplying, but nowhere so sharply as in the United States. A survey there a few years ago showed that there were 35 million cats and 48 million dogs. But a further investigation in 1987 revealed that the totals had risen to 56.2 million cats and 51 million dogs. In other words, the increase in the number of dogs has merely been keeping pace with the growth in the human population, but the figure for cats has risen dramatically and for the first time they outnumber 'man's best friend'.

American sociologists have been intrigued by 'The Attack of the Cat People', as one Californian writer headlined the upsurge in addiction to felines, and have been searching for explanations. Some see it as a reflection of the number of owners who have to go out to work; or the increase in lonely people living by themselves; or the modern reluctance of many young couples to have children too soon. Others stress the rise in numbers of elderly people in the population, or the further shift towards apartment-dwelling.

In all these cases, cats have advantages over dogs. The

house-pets of working owners must be content with hours every day spent on their own, and cats do not mind being left alone in the home, whereas dogs crave non-stop company. Dogs need more space, so apartment-dwellers also find cats more suitable in the home. And dogs are always pleading for long walks, something that the elderly cannot always give them, much as they would like to.

These factors may explain most of the rise in feline popularity, but some observers feel that there is an additional, hidden influence that has to do with the changing social mood of recent years. They detect a growing respect for individualism and a decline in mindless loyalties to our major institutions. Respect for authority, they say, is more and more difficult to drum up with the usual slogans and ceremonies. It is still there, of course, but with it there is a cynical tinge – a wry smile that says 'we will follow you, but in our own way, and really we cannot take you too seriously'. The politicians, priests and pundits may still be our social leaders, but now, instead of looking up to them, we spend more time looking down at their clay feet. All of this sounds much more like a feline relationship than a canine one. Dogs are loyal slaves, ready for action to aid the pack. Cats are independent and individualistic, tolerating our leadership but not respecting it. They therefore reflect the new social mood of the human community and our co-existence with them suits that mood perfectly. We admire in them what we feel growing in ourselves.

Connected with this change is a significant shift in animal literature. Quirky cats have replaced heroic dogs in childrens' stories to a striking degree. And it is *Cats* not *Dogs* that are starring on stage at present in the West End of London and Broadway in New York.

It is a sobering thought that in the United States the figure for cat food sales, which has doubled in the last eight years to an astonishing $2 billion a year, now exceeds that for baby food. In weight, Americans are now buying 2.25 billion pounds of cat food each year – not to mention a million tons of cat litter. There is no doubt about it – we are clearly living in the Age of the Cat.

* * * *

This was brought home to me last year when I had a book called *Catwatching* published. In it I tried to answer all the basic questions about cat behaviour that I had, as a zoologist, been studying over the years. Answers to such seemingly simple questions as 'Why does a cat purr?' or 'Why does a cat wag its tail?' were not as straightforward as most people seemed to imagine. The reaction to the book astonished me. It became a bestseller on both sides of the Atlantic and I was inundated with many new feline questions to which cat owners were demanding answers. I was fascinated by the great variety of these queries and set about investigating them and answering them. It soon became clear that effectively I was writing another book, hence the present volume, *Catlore*, which could be described as an advanced course in catwatching.

Sadly, I have not been able to deal with all the questions that have been posed to me. 'What does my cat dream about?' is something we will never be able to answer. We know for certain that they do dream and, judging by the sounds and twitches they make while doing so, there is a great deal of feline courtship and mouse-killing going on, but this is mere guesswork and has no place in a book that struggles to be as scientific and objective about cats as it is possible to be.

Some questions produce answers that are too short to make into interesting chapters, such as the extraordinary query: 'Is it true that a tom-cat with bad teeth can never become a father?' (Yes, because he will not be able to cling on to the female's neck with his teeth when he is mating with her and without that ability he will never be able to mount her successfully.)

Others I am still investigating and will require a great deal more research before they can be answered satisfactorily. The most common of these is an old chestnut: 'What is the difference between a cat owner and a dog owner?' I have been asked this repeatedly and have given a number of oversimplified answers that have suited the mood of the moment – artists prefer cats, soldiers prefer dogs; introverts prefer cats, extroverts prefer dogs; rebels prefer cats, authoritarians prefer dogs; and so on. There is an element of truth in all these statements, but how big an element? What is needed is a serious investigation into the differences between cat people and dog people. Because there *are* differences between them, but they are inevitably much more subtle and complex than my simple contrasts suggest. There is a detailed survey waiting to be done and its results, I predict, will prove most intriguing. For there is no doubt that our companion animals do reflect our personalities and lifestyles to a remarkable degree.

In the meantime here are my answers to fifty of the questions that fascinated me the most. Where I did not already know the answers, I have learned a great deal in my pursuit of them and, in the process, I have come to respect cats even more than I did at the outset. What graceful, complicated, infuriating, delightful animals they are, and what a privilege it is to be able to share a room, or a life, with one of them.

Yet how some tyrants loathed them. Alexander the Great, Napoleon and Hitler were all fanatical cat-haters. They may have led great armies and slaughtered millions, but they were apparently terrified of small felines. Nothing could underline better the nature of the cat's extraordinary presence. If you want to conquer the world you had better not share even a moment with an animal that refuses to be conquered at any price, by anyone.

How sensitive is the cat's hearing?

The cat's ears are much more sensitive than those of its owners, which is why cats loathe noisy homes. Loud music, screaming and shouting are torture to the delicate hearing apparatus of the typical feline.

It is the specialized hunting behaviour of cats that has resulted in their improved hearing. Although dogs have a much greater acoustic range than humans, cats exceed even dogs in their ability to hear high-pitched sounds. This is because humans and dogs rely most on chasing and trapping their prey, whereas cats prefer to lurk in ambush and listen very carefully for the tiniest sound. If they are to succeed as stealthy hunters, they must be able to detect the most minute rustlings and squeaks, and must be able to distinguish precise direction and distance to pinpoint their intended victims. This requires much more sensitivity than we possess, and laboratory tests have confirmed that domestic cats do, indeed, possess a very fine tuning ability.

At the lower level of sounds, there is little difference between humans, dogs and cats – this is not where it counts, if you are a hunter of small rodents and birds. At the higher levels, humans in the prime of life can hear noises up to about 20,000 cycles per second. This sinks to around 12,000 cycles per second in humans of retirement age. Dogs can manage up to 35,000 to 40,000 cycles per second, so that they are able to detect sounds that we cannot. Cats, on the other hand, can hear sounds up to an astonishing 100,000 cycles per second. This corresponds well to the high pitch of mouse sounds, which can be emitted up to this same level. So no mouse is safe from the alert ears of the predatory cat.

Opinions differ as to how high the cat can hear at full sensitivity. Some authorities believe that a really delicate reaction is only possible for the domestic cat at up to 45,000 cycles per second. Above this, they feel, there is a much weaker response. Most experts agree, however, that the figure is nearer 60,000 to 65,000 cycles per second, which would be enough to hear most prey sounds.

This acoustic ability of pet cats explains why they sometimes appear to have supernatural powers. They hear and understand the ultrasonic sounds that precede a noisy activity and respond appropriately before we have even realized that something unusual is going to happen. And do not overlook the ability of your snoozing feline. Even while taking a catnap the animal's ears are in operation. If something exciting is detected the cat is awake and responding in a split second. Perhaps this is why it sleeps twice as long as we do, making up in length of slumber what it lacks in depth.

Sadly for old cats, this wonderful sensitivity does not last forever. By the age of about five years a cat starts to lose its range of hearing and when the animal has become elderly, in feline terms, it is often nearly deaf. This explains why old cats sometimes fall victim to fast cars. It is not that they are too slow to avoid being hit, but that they simply do not hear the cars speeding towards them.

Younger cats are not only good at hearing high-pitched squeaks, they are also brilliant at detecting precise direction. They can distinguish between two sounds which are only 18 inches apart at a distance of 60 feet; they can separate with ease two sounds that are coming from the same direction, but at different distances; and they can differentiate two sounds that have only a half-tone of difference between them. In some tests this last ability was shown to one-tenth of a tone. Human composers must envy the cat its ears. But it is sad for the ordinary cat owner to realize that there is a whole range of sounds that simply cannot be shared with a much-loved pet. It is one of the humbling lessons we learn from living with companion animals, namely that we are in so many ways their inferiors, even though as a species we have come to dominate the planet.

How do cats react to music?

The correct answer appears to be idiosyncratically. Some cats show no interest whatever, while others detest it and still others adore it. It is hard, at first, to make any sense out of the reports that exist in the feline literature.

The French writer Theophile Gautier, for example, observed that his female cat would always listen attentively to the singers that he accompanied on the piano. She was not happy, however, when high notes were struck. They probably reminded her too closely of sounds of feline distress and she did her best to silence them. Whenever a female singer reached a high A, the cat would reach out and close the songstress's mouth with her paw. There must have been something specially feline about that particular note, because Gautier carried out experiments to see if he could fool the cat, but she always responded with her critical paw precisely when the note reached high A.

A more severe music critic was one of the cats owned by Frenchman C.C. Pierquin de Gembloux. This animal's reaction to certain sequences of notes was to throw itself into uncontrollable convulsions. A second cat, present at the same time, responded in a totally different way. Instead of having a fit, it jumped up and sat on the piano, listening to the same music with great interest.

The composer Henri Sauguet was astonished to discover that his cat, Cody, became ecstatic when it heard Debussy being played on the piano. It would roll around on the carpet, then leap on to the piano and then on to the pianist's lap, where it would start licking the hands that played the magic notes. When these same hands gave up playing under the onslaught of feline affection, the cat would wander off, but if they then began to play again, the cat immediately dashed back and resumed its licking.

Back in the 1930s two doctors by the names of Morin and Bachrach discovered to their surprise that the note of E of the

7

fourth octave had the effect of making young cats defecate and adult ones become sexually excited. It was also noted that extremely high notes caused agitation in many cats.

What are we to deduce from these remarkable observations? Why on earth should cats have any reactions at all to something as sophisticated as human music? The answer seems to lie with the special signals that are given in feline 'language' by certain specific sounds. The mewing of a distressed kitten, for instance, is at a particular pitch, and if a musical note hits that pitch then it will disturb an adult cat, especially a female one. This may explain why Gautier's cat touched the mouths of the singers with her paw when they hit the particular note. She must have thought, at that moment, that each singer was a 'kitten' in distress, and she was no doubt trying to help in her own way.

Similarly, Sauguet's cat probably thought that his owner needed help, and rushed over to lick the hands from which the sounds seemed to be coming, as a way of comforting him – just as a mother cat would rush across to lick the fur of one of its kittens if the young animal appeared to be in distress.

The convulsions and sexual excitement of other cats are probably no more than erotic responses to sounds that remind felines of the courtship tones of their species. And fear induced by very high-pitched musical notes could simply be the natural panic reaction to what the cat hears as squeals of pain.

In other words, the musical sense of cats is just another feline myth. All they are doing – and with some remarkable individual variation – is responding to selected notes from the great array that music offers them, according to their own instinctive system of sound signals. Some musical notes trigger off parental feelings, others sexual ones and still others self-protection. The cats are mistaking our messages and we, in the past, have reciprocated by misunderstanding theirs.

How does a cat purr?

It comes as a surprise to most people to learn that the experts are still arguing over something as basic as how a cat purrs. It is even more unexpected to find that the two alternative explanations are completely different from one another. This is not a dispute over some small detail, but about the basic mechanism of purring. Here are the rival theories:

The *false vocal cord* theory sees purring originating in the cat's voice-box, or larynx. In addition to the ordinary vocal cords, the cat possesses a second pair of structures called vestibular folds, or false vocal cords. The presence of this second pair of cords is thought to be the secret behind the extraordinary purring mechanism that permits the animal to produce the soft, rumbling sound for minutes and even hours on end, without any effort and without opening the mouth.

This theory regards purring as little more than heavy breathing of the type humans sometimes indulge in when they are asleep – in other words, snoring. With every inhalation and exhalation, air passes over the false vocal cords and makes the rrrrrrr noise of the purr. To produce this characteristic sound, air has to be interrupted by the contraction of the laryngeal muscles about thirty times a second.

The *turbulent blood* theory says that the cat's voice-box has nothing whatever to do with purring. Instead, it is argued that when the cat's blood-flow through its main veins into the heart is increased, turbulence is created. This is greatest at the point where the main vein, carrying blood from the animal's body back into its heart, is constricted as it passes through the animal's chest. The swirling blood is thought to make the purring noise, the diaphram acting as an amplifier of the vibrations. The noise thus created is thought to be passed up the animal's windpipe and into the sinus cavities of the skull, where it resonates to produce the purring sound. Some authorities believe that it is the arching of the back of the purring cat that increases this blood turbulence to create the

9

purring sound, while others see the increase as being more to do with emotional changes affecting the animal's blood flow.

To the non-specialist there seems little doubt as to which of these theories provides the correct explanation. The false vocal cord theory is the most obvious and the simplest. It explains the otherwise puzzling presence of the second, or false, pair of vocal cords. We know that the true vocal cords are the ones that produce the ordinary vocalizations of the cat, such as miaowing, yowling and screaming, and if the false cords do not produce purring, then their presence requires some other explanation.

The blood turbulence theory has the merit of ingenuity, but little else. Anyone who has listened to a cat purring, using a stethoscope, will agree that when strongly amplified in this way, the purring sound simply does not have the quality of resonating blood turbulence. It is far too vibratory. And the idea that postural or emotional changes could bring on purring also seems far-fetched. The purring animal is relaxed, and common sense demands that this is precisely the time when any blood turbulence would subside, not increase.

Finally, the false vocal cord theory is supported by the evidence of the simple action of placing your fingers gently on the throat of a purring cat – there is no doubt, then, that the purring sound is stemming from the region of the voice-box, and it is hard to see why any alternative theory should have been put forward. That it *has*, despite the fact that superficially it is so unlikely, should, however, keep us on our toes. In biology, the most obvious explanation is not always the correct one, and much 'obvious' evidence has been disproved by careful, modern research. Where purring cats are concerned we must continue to keep an open mind.

How many sounds does a cat make?

A blind musician claimed that he could detect a hundred different sounds made by cats. American research workers, studying many hours of tape recordings, also insist that the feline vocal repertoire is huge – the most complex of any animal except *Homo sapiens*. Why should this be, when the wild cat is not a particularly sociable animal? In nature, it is those species that live in highly organized groups that require the most complicated communication systems. So there seems to be something odd about the cat.

The explanation is that the domestic cat uses two vocabularies at once. In the wild it would have one set of sounds for the mother–offspring relationship and would then replace that with another set for adult life. In the human home, the tame cat retains its infant vocalizations right through into adulthood and improves on them in the process. In addition, it also has all the usual howls and wails of the adult feline world of sex and violence. Put together this makes a truly impressive vocabulary.

Another way in which the cat's sound system appears much more complex than that of other species is in the degree of variation that can be applied to a single type of call. For a bird, an alarm call may be just a whistle and always that whistle. If the bird becomes more and more agitated, it simply repeats the whistle more often and perhaps faster. But when a cat is upset it can produce a whole variety of miaowing calls that sound different enough from one another to be classified as distinct vocalizations.

The danger with accepting that cats have a hundred different sounds is that the whole subject becomes too complicated to make much sense. The way of avoiding this is not to list all the sounds, but rather to list the signals or messages that the cat is trying to convey to its companions. When this is done, the language of the cat becomes much more clear. Here are some of the main messages and the noises that transmit them:

11

1 'I am angry'

When cats fight there is a terrible din. Since Chaucer's day this has been referred to as CATERWAULING, but it is often recorded not as an aggressive sound but as a sexual one. This error is found even in the august Oxford English Dictionary, where to caterwaul has been defined as 'To make the noise proper to cats at rutting time'. In fact, the sound is heard at any time when two cats are fighting and may have nothing whatever to do with sexual encounters. Two spayed females disputing a territorial boundary can caterwaul as dramatically as any 'rutting toms'.

The reason why caterwauling is associated with rutting is because it is most common then, the scent of the female on heat attracting males from far and wide and bringing them uncomfortably close together, so that they feel unusually inclined to vent their feelings of hostility towards one another.

The caterwauling of an aggressive cat is a perfect example of a single signal that takes many different forms. Each of these forms, or intensities, can be given a separate name, but they all belong to the same basic message: 'Clear off, or I will attack you.' Because the vocalization is prolonged and because the mood of hostility rises and falls second by second, the strength of the sound increases and decreases as well. As it does so, instead of simply becoming louder or softer, it changes its whole quality. Because of this, people speak of cats GROWLING, SNARLING, GURGLING, WAILING and HOWLING, to give just a few of the names that have been attached to this belligerent kind of sound production. All of these are varying intensities of the same basic sound unit and should be treated as such.

2 'I am frightened'

When a cat is afraid, its normal reaction is to run away silently, or to hide. There is no point in making a lot of noise at such a moment. But if a cat is cornered and cannot run away, even though it wishes fervently to do so, it may then make a sound which transmits the message: 'I fear you, but do not push me too far, or I will turn on you despite my fear.' A cat in such a situation may perform a strange, throaty YOWLING noise. This indicates that although it is very scared it has not entirely lost its aggression. Pressed further, it will lash out. More commonly, it will perform the SPIT and HISS display, especially if its tormentor is a large dog or an aggressive human being. Viewed objectively, these are strange sounds to offer an attacker. They are not very loud and in terms of the volume of sound produced they are not particularly impressive. And yet they do seem to work remarkably well, putting even the largest dog into a suddenly more respectful mood. There is a special reason for the sounds. Many mammals have an inborn fear of poisonous snakes and the defensive noises of a cornered snake are, of course, the spit and hiss. So the cat is almost certainly performing a mimicry display, reacting like a snake in the hope of triggering off some deep-seated fear of a venomous bite in the assailant's mind.

3 'I am in pain'

The SCREAM of a cat in agony is unmistakable and is similar to the scream of many other animals when being badly hurt or terrorized. It is sometimes described as a SHRIEK or a SCREECH, according to its intensity, and it is an adult version of the SQUEAL of a distressed kitten. For the kitten, it acts as a vital signal to its mother to come to the rescue. For the adult, it no longer provokes much help, since there is little mutual aid between adult felines, but where pet cats are involved it can, of course, act as a useful signal to the cat's pseudo-parents – its human owners – who may then, like surrogate mother cats, come to its rescue.

A special context in which the pain signal is given is at the end of the mating act, when the tom-cat is withdrawing his barbed penis from the female. This tears her and causes her a sharp pang of pain, making her cry out. Although pain is the dominant feeling she experiences at that moment, it is a pain that simultaneously makes her angry with the male, and she swipes out at him. The combination of acute pain with sudden hostility produces a harsher version of the usual cry of pain – more of a screech than a scream. The male reads it loud and clear and quickly attempts to avoid the sharp claws that are lunging towards him.

4 'I want attention'

For cat owners this is the most familiar sound to emanate from their feline friends. The MIAOW says many things in many contexts, but it always has the same basic message, namely 'I require your immediate attention'. It originates as a MEWING sound in tiny kittens, letting their mother know that they need some kind of help or that they are in some sort of trouble. In wild cats it then more or less disappears as they become adult, but domestic cats remain mentally like kittens even when they are fully grown, and continue to 'talk' to their human owners like kittens communicating with their mothers. And they do more. They start to refine their miaows in a way that wild cats never seem to do. They take the infantile mewing and they modify it to each situation in which they wish to express a need for something. There are begging miaows and demanding miaows, complaining miaows and anxious miaows. There are soft, flat miaows to be let out of the house and pitiful, drawn-out miaows to be let in again when it starts raining. There are expectant miaows when tin-opener noises are detected and irritated miaows when some fixed routine has been disregarded. An alert owner will know each of these variants on the 'I want attention' signal and may become quite fluent in 'cat-ese' after a few years.

Brave attempts have been made by certain experts to write down the different miaows, in order to classify and standardize them. The results are often hilarious, as when we are asked to distinguish between the MHRHRNAAAAHOU, the MHRHRHRN-NAAAAHOOOUUU and the MHHNGAAHOU. The human alphabet simply cannot cope, and unless you know the sounds already (in which case there is no point in writing them down) there is no hope of learning them from these strange strings of letters. Furthermore, since the refinement of the different miaows as your pet cat grows older is a personal affair between you and the cat, it is not surprising that there is considerable variation from one animal to another. They all start with the basic feline sound, genetically inherited like all the other elements of their communication system, but the artificial nature of the adult cat/human owner relationship creates a special world in which new subtleties develop that go beyond the genetically-shared vocabulary. Feline individualism begins to assert itself, and anyone who has owned, say, a crossbred tabby, a Siamese, a Persian and an Abyssinian will know that not only different individuals but also different breeds have their own special vocal characteristics. It would require a feline Professor Higgins to unravel all the intricacies of the language of the modern domesticated cat.

5 'Come with me'

When a mother cat wants her kittens to come near to her or to follow her, she gives a soft little CHIRRUPING noise. She may also use it as a greeting when she has been away from the kittens for a while. Adult domestic cats employ this same signal, which has been accurately described as a 'rising trill', when they are greeting their human owners. At such moments they are reversing the usual relationship and treating the humans as their kittens rather than as their mothers. (They also do this when they bring their owners dead birds from the garden, an action normally done only as part of the food-training routine when mother cats show their kittens the kind of prey they must later attack.) Significantly, the greeting trill is normally done when they are on the move, usually when they have come in from outside and are about to move off towards the place where they expect food to be waiting. So, although it sounds like a greeting, it probably still has some of the 'come along, follow me' meaning in it.

6 'I am inoffensive'

This is the famous feline PURRING sound. It is hard for some owners to accept that this noise means 'I am inoffensive' rather than 'I am content', but the fact is that inoffensiveness is the only condition to explain all the different contexts in which the purr occurs. It is essentially a signal that says the cat is in a non-hostile mood, is friendly, submissive, reassuring, appeasing, or, of course, contented. It is observed in the following cat-to-cat situations:

a   When kittens are sucking at the nipple, letting the mother know all is well.
b   When the mother is lying with her kittens, reassuring them that all is well.
c   When the mother approaches the nest where the kittens are hiding, letting them know that there is nothing to fear by her approach.
d   When a young cat approaches an adult for play, letting it

15

know that it is in a relaxed mood and accepts its subordinate social position.

e When a dominant adult cat approaches a young cat in a friendly way, reassuring it of its non-hostile intentions.

f When an inferior cat is approached by a dominant enemy, as an attempt to appease the more powerful one with its submissive, non-hostile signal.

g When a sick cat is approached by a dominant one, letting it know that it is in a weak, non-hostile mood.

Again, attempts have been made to classify purrs into different types, but they all carry the same basic message of friendliness. The nearest human equivalent to purring is smiling, and we also make the same mistake when we say that a smiling man is a happy man. Just like purring, smiling can occur when we are being reassuring, submissive, non-hostile, and appeasing, as well as when we are blissfully happy. Like the purr, the key message of the smile is 'I am NOT going to do you any harm'. As such it is vitally important for 'softening' social relationships and de-stressing moments of close proximity.

7 *'I want to sink my teeth into you'*

There is a strange little CLICKING noise made by cats that are on the prowl and have spotted a prey animal. They use a variant of it, a sort of teeth-gnashing, when they see a bird through a window. It is no more than the action of clashing their teeth together as if sinking them into the neck of the prey, in the specialized killing bite of the cat, but it has become a sound signal that many observers have commented on. Some authors have suggested that the clicks are made to alert other cats to the presence of the prey. One even made the mistake of describing it as a signal to 'alert others in the pack', as if cats are group-hunting animals like wolves. The fact that cats are solitary hunters and would certainly not wish to let other felines join them in stalking a particular prey, makes this clicking noise something of a mystery. The only possible explanation is that it is employed by mother cats when out with their nearly fully-grown kittens, to help focus their attention on potential prey, as part of a general hunt-training process.

These are the seven most important sound messages made by

domestic cats. With their many variants and subdivisions they provide a wonderfully expressive earful for the alert feline as it goes about its business. For human cat owners they offer a fascinatingly rich field of study and access to the world of their feline companions. Only occasionally do they jar on the nerves, as when your queen on heat starts her pitiful calling ('I want attention' – of a special kind) and attracts a chorus of savagely competitive, caterwauling toms to the space beneath your bedroom window. But the next time this happens, instead of hurling buckets of water, switch on a tape recorder and then, the next day, sit down and enjoy the feline opera at your leisure. If your sleep is not at risk, you will find the amazingly complicated sequence of moans, growls and yowls an absorbing example of prolonged animal communication.

What does a cat signal with its eyes?

The next time you feed your cat, take a close look at its eyes. If it is hungry, the moment the food dish appears the animal's pupils will dilate. The vertical slits will expand to dark pools of feline expectation. Careful tests have shown that when this happens the area of the pupils may increase to between four and five times their previous size in less than one second.

This dramatic change is part of the cat's mood-signalling system, but it is only one way in which the eyes change their expression. The most basic eye change is connected with variations in light intensity. The more light that falls on the eyes, the more the pupils contract to vertical slits; the less light there is, the more they open up to round, black pools. This type of alteration in the appearance of the eye goes on all day, as the animal moves from light to shade and back again, and it is so common a shift that it tends to obscure the other pupil changes that are taking place.

Proximity of the viewed scene also affects the cat's pupils: the closer an object is, the more it has to constrict them; with more distant objects it expands them a little. This type of change also interferes with our reading of the mood-signals coming from the eyes.

To make matters even more complicated, there are two quite distinct kinds of mood-change, for the cat's pupils will become greatly enlarged not only when it sees something pleasant but also when it sees something terribly threatening. The only way to clarify this state of affairs is to say that if you see a cat's pupils suddenly expand, without any change in light intensity or proximity of objects, then it is experiencing a state of strong emotional arousal. This arousal may be pleasant, as with the arrival of tasty food, or unpleasant, as with the arrival of a large aggressive rival. In both cases, the pupils will enlarge more than normal, as if trying to increase the input of information from the exciting stimuli.

Because a frightened, defensive cat shows extreme pupil

expansion, an opposite signal seems to have evolved for its dominant, aggressive and fearless rival. For such an animal there is only one possible kind of eye expression: the narrow vertical slit of a fully contracted pupil. But take care! This does not mean that only a slit-eyed cat is dangerous. A frightened cat with expanded pupils is just as likely to strike out in panic. In fact, a submissive cat in the house that has 'had enough' and is about to defend itself will often dilate its pupils rapidly just before it lashes out at you. So it is important to read the 'expanded pupil' signal very carefully and to place it in context before interpreting it.

In addition to pupil changes there is also the possibility of signalling mood by the degree of opening or closing the eyelids. An alert cat has fully-opened eyes and this is the condition that is always maintained in the presence of strangers, who are not entirely trusted by the cat. If the animal switches to half-closed eyes, this is an expression of total relaxation signalling complete trust in the friendship of its owners.

Full closure of the eyes only occurs in two contexts: sleep and appeasement. When two cats are fighting and one is forced into submission, it often performs what is called 'cut-off', where it turns away from its tormentor and shuts its eyes, trying to blot out the frightening image of its dominant rival. This is basically a protective action, an attempt to save the eyes from possible danger, but it has also become a way of reducing the unbearable tension of the moment. In addition, the victor sees it as a sign of capitulation by his opponent.

Finally a word about the stare. Prolonged staring with wide-open eyes has a special significance for the cat. It is an eye signal that denotes aggression. In other words, for a human being to stare at a cat is to threaten it. Yet we are always doing this, because we so like to enjoy contemplating the beauty of our feline companions. We do it innocently, without wishing the cat any harm, but it is sometimes difficult for the animal to appreciate this. The solution is to enjoy staring at the cat at moments when it is not staring back. If we lock eyes with it we are unavoidably intimidating it, when this is the last thing we wish to do. By a small adjustment, however, we can greatly improve our relationship and make the cat feel much more comfortable and at ease in our presence.

How many tail-signals does a cat make?

In addition to the familiar tail-wagging of a cat in a conflict, there are a number of other tail-signals that indicate the changing moods of the pet feline as it goes about its business. Each tail movement or posture tells us (and other cats) something about the animal's emotional condition and it is possible to draw up a 'de-coding key', as follows:

Tail curves gently down and then up again at the tip
  This is the relaxed cat, at peace with the world.
Tail raised slightly and softly curved
  The cat is becoming interested in something.
Tail held erect but with the tip tilted over
  The cat is very interested and is in a friendly, greeting mood, but with slight reservations.
Tail fully erect with the tip stiffly vertical
  An intense greeting display with no reservations. In adult cats, this posture is 'borrowed' from the action of a kitten greeting its mother. The kitten's signal is an invitation to the mother cat to inspect its rear end, so there is an element of subordination in this display, as there is in most greeting ceremonies.
Tail lowered fully and possibly even tucked between the hind legs
  This is the signal of a defeated or totally submissive cat that wishes to stress its lowly social status.
Tail lowered and fluffed out
  The cat is indicating active fear.
Tail swished violently from side to side
  This is the conflict signal of tail-wagging, in its most angry version. If the tail swings very vigorously from side to side it usually means that the animal is about to attack, if it can summon up that last ounce of aggression.
Tail held still, but with tip twitching
  This is the version of tail-wagging that indicates only mild irritation. But if the tip-twitching becomes more power-

ful, then it can act as a clue that a swipe from a bad-tempered paw is imminent.

Tail held erect with its whole length quivered

This gentle quivering action is often seen after a cat has been greeted by its owner. It is the same action that is observed when urine-spraying is taking place out of doors, but in this case there is no urine produced. Whether some slight, invisible scent is expelled is not clear, but the gesture appears to have the meaning of a friendly 'personal identification' as if the cat is saying, 'Yes, this is *me*!'

Tail held to one side

This is the sexual invitation signal of the female cat on heat. When she is ready to be mounted by the male she conspicuously moves her tail over to one side. When he sees this, the tom-cat knows he can mount her without being attacked.

Tail held straight and fully bristled

This is the signal of an aggressive cat.

Tail arched and bristled

This is the signal of a defensive cat, but one that may attack if provoked further. The bristling of the fur makes the animal look bigger, a 'transformation display' that may deter the enemy if the defensive cat is lucky.

Do cats have ESP?

Many people believe that cats are capable of some kind of extra-sensory perception, but they are not. It has become popular to explain anything puzzling as being due to some supernatural power, but this is a short cut to complacency. The scientific truth is often much more fascinating, but investigating it is stifled if we simply relegate every unusual occurrence to the dustbin of 'mystic forces'.

To start with, ESP is a contradiction in terms. Anything we perceive is, by definition, something which operates through one of our sense organs. So, if something is extra-sensory it cannot be perceived. Therefore there cannot be any such thing as ESP.

If a cat performs some very strange action – finds its way home over a long distance, predicts an earthquake, or senses the return of its owners when they are some distance from the house – then it is a challenge for us to try and find out which particular sensory pathway was involved. To put the feat down to ESP is boring, because it simply stops any further enquiry. It says the cat has magical powers, and that is an end to it. Much more stimulating is the idea that everything cats (or humans for that matter) do is capable of logical explanation, if only we can find out how the behaviour mechanism operates.

If we find that magnets attached to cats will upset their ability to find their way home, then we are beginning, very dimly, to understand the amazing homing abilities that the animals have evolved over a long period of time. If we find that cats are sensitive to very small vibrations or changes in the static electricity of their environment, then we might come to understand how they can predict earthquakes. And if we can learn more about their sensitivity to ultrasonic sounds, we may finally grasp how they can 'know' that someone is approaching from a great distance.

This does not mean that we will be able to explain everything a cat does. We may have to wait for much more advanced technology before we can do that. But ultimately it should be possible and the 'mysterious cat' will be mysterious no more. And if and when this happens, the cat will, because of our detailed knowledge of its abilities, be more fascinating to us than ever before. To explain something is not to explain it away and to understand something is not to underestimate its value.

Against all this the ESP addicts will retort that there is one feat performed by some cats that requires an acceptance of telepathic communication between human owner and lost feline. This is the 'psychic trailing' phenomenon, when a cat that has been left behind by its owners follows them to their *new* home. There are cases where owners genuinely believe that their pet cat has followed them by some mystical means to a new home several thousand miles away from the original one. The cats in question have never lived near the new home and do not have any knowledge of the new locality. Yet they turn up again, mewing to their astonished owners, sometimes as long as two years after being accidently left at the old home site. Explain this, the ESP devotees will say, and we will withdraw our case.

If it were true it would be a remarkable telepathic phenomenon, but sadly there is usually a much simpler explanation. The world is full of stray cats, many of them searching hopefully for a new home. Anyone living in a house without a cat is likely to be visited by a stray sooner or later. There are only so many different varieties of coat colour for moggies, and if the family cat was a tabby, or a black cat with a white flash on its chest, then the owners are not to be blamed for thinking that their long-lost friend has finally found its way home. If this sounds cynical, it is not difficult to set up a simple experiment. Take a cat and place it in a special room with a circle of passages and doors. Have different people behind each door at the end of each passageway and see if the cat heads towards the door hiding its owners, ignoring the other doors with strangers behind them. When rigorous experimenting of this kind is done, the telepathic results are disappointing. So these simple tests are usually avoided by the ESP enthusiasts, who would romantically prefer the cat to remain a mystic feline force among us.

How delicate is the cat's sense of taste?

Since cats can see, hear and smell with more sensitivity than we can, it is reassuring to find that in one respect at least we have superior sense organs. When it comes to taste, our tongues are slightly better than theirs. But only slightly. Like us, cats are responsive to four basic tastes – sour, bitter, salt and sweet. We respond to all four strongly, but cats are weak when it comes to sweet tastes. They lack our 'sweet tooth'.

Until recently many authorities stated categorically that cats, almost alone among mammals, were incapable of detecting sweet tastes. One said, without qualification, 'The cat shows no response to sweet tastes.' Another declared, 'Sweet tastes cannot be discerned by the cat.' This traditional wisdom must now be discarded. New tests have proved conclusively that cats *can* appreciate the presence of sweet tastes. If milk is diluted to one quarter of its normal strength, and hungry cats are then offered a choice between this weak milk laced with sucrose against the same milk without any sweetening, they always prefer the sweetened dishes.

If this is the case, why has it been denied in the past? The answer is that in most tests cats ignore the sweetness factor when making choices. It is of such minor significance to them that they 'override' it. If, for example, they are tested with full-strength or even half-strength milk, they show no preference for the more or the less sweetened examples. Their reaction to the milk itself is too strong. Only when the milk factor is greatly reduced by dilution does the sweetness factor begin to show. So although cats do enjoy this taste, they do so at a very mild level indeed.

Their strongest reaction is to sour tastes; next comes bitter, then salt and finally sweet. As food touches the tongue it comes into contact with the sensory papillae there. In the middle of the tongue these papillae are strong, rough and backward-pointing. In this area, there is a specialization of the tongue's surface that has nothing to do with taste. Indeed, there are no taste buds in this central region. It is a zone concerned entirely with rasping meat from bones or with cleaning fur. The taste buds are confined to the tip, the sides and the back of the tongue only. Sour tastes can be detected in all these areas, but bitter is confined to the back part and salt to the front.

However, the most powerful response of all to the food is to its smell, or fragrance. This is the really important information cats are receiving when they approach a meal. It is why many will sniff it and then walk away without even attempting to taste it. Like a wine connoisseur who only has to sniff the vintage to know how good it is, a cat can learn all it wants to know without actually trying the food.

If the animal does take a mouthful, then the tongue also has a sensitive reaction to the food's temperature. The wild ancestors of our domestic cats liked to eat freshly killed prey – they were not scavengers. And the tame descendants have kept the same views on this matter. The ideal, preferred temperature for feline food is 86°F, which happens to be the same temperature as the cat's tongue. Food taken straight from the refrigerator is anathema to the cat – unless it is very hungry, in which case it will eat almost anything. Sadly, for most cats today heated food is something of a luxury and, like many humans, they have learned to live with the 'fast food' mentality of modern times.

Why do cats sometimes reject their food?

Every cat owner knows the moment when a pet approaches a new dish of food, sniffs it, and then stalks off without taking a bite. It does not happen often, but when it does it is puzzling. Why should the cat suddenly refuse food that it normally eats with great enthusiasm?

Could the cat be ill? Yes, but this is not the explanation in many cases, where the animal is perfectly healthy in all other respects.

Could the food be bad? Yes, but again this cannot be the whole story because sometimes the food in question is identical to the previous meal, which was consumed greedily. Some owners have observed that two helpings of exactly the same cat food, given at different times on the same day, are treated differently – the first being eaten, the second rejected.

If the cat is well and the food is good, then what we are dealing with is a problem in feline behaviour, and any of a number of factors may be operating.

One explanation is that cats prefer to eat small meals on frequent occasions, rather than gorge on large, infrequent meals. Considering the size of their natural prey – small mice and birds – this is not so surprising. Unfortunately for domestic cats, their human owners rarely have the time to offer them mouse-sized meals, preferring to spoon out big dishfuls of cat food at feeding times. If you compare the amount of meat on an ordinary mouse with the amount of meat you place in your pet's food dish, you will find that the average cat-meal is about the equivalent of five mice. Although this is convenient for busy human owners, it is too much for the cat to eat at once, unless it is starving – which is rarely the case with well-loved family pets. Usually the cat eats a mouse-worth of food and then strolls off to digest it, returning later for another rodent-sized portion, and so on, until all the food is gone.

On this basis, if one meal is eaten and the dish emptied, and then the next meal is refused, it may simply be that the cat is not yet ready for its next 'kill'. Cats are normally extremely efficient at regulating the amount of food they take in. Obese cats are far less common than obese dogs (or obese people). So if they are being slightly overfed they may occasionally rebel and leave a new dish of food untouched.

Once again, this cannot be the complete story, because some owners have observed that their pets' daily intake is not always the same. On certain days the cats suddenly decide to eat much less than usual. Why should this be? One explanation is that sex is about to rear its head. If you have a female cat and it is coming into heat, it may temporarily go off its food, for example. Alternatively, if the weather suddenly becomes hotter or more humid, or both, cats may instantly cut down on their food intake.

Another possibility is that, unknown to you, your cat may be obtaining food elsewhere. A friendly neighbour may be giving titbits when visited by your roaming pet, which then returns home with its appetite ruined. Or there may have been a sudden and unexpected explosion in the local mouse population, leading to a spate of hunting and killing by a pet cat that normally feeds only at home. Again, its appetite will be dramatically reduced without any warning, leaving a perplexed owner to scrape a pile of stale cat food into the dustbin.

Another, less likely, possibility is that your cat hates the place in which it is given its food dish. Cats do not like to eat in a spot where there is bright light, a great deal of noise, or a lot of busy movement. They prefer to devour their 'prey' in a quiet, dim, private corner, away from the hustle and bustle of the home. Given an unsuitable feeding place, they may become erratic in their response to food. If they are unusually anxious or irritated, they may find the noise just too much to deal with and stalk off in a feline sulk rather than squat down for a good meal. Whether they eat or not in such cases will depend not so much on the food itself as on their varying mood.

Finally, even if all the factors mentioned so far are *not* influencing the cat, it may still turn its nose up at a particular dish of food. In such instances there is an inborn 'food variety mechanism' operating. This was originally discovered in birds, where seed-eaters were seen to switch from one type of seed to another from time to time, regardless of the nutritional similarity of the seeds. Given just one type of seed, they would always eat it and be perfectly healthy. They did not suffer from an unchanging diet. But if they were then given a choice of several kinds of seeds they would show sudden switches in preference, even though the seeds were chemically much the same. In the wild the importance of this mechanism is that it prevents a bird from becoming totally 'hooked' on one kind of foodstuff, so that if that type of seed suddenly disappears it is not left stranded. With wild cats it ensures that the animals do not become totally dependent on one kind of prey. With domestic cats it means that, every so often, the old 'standby' diet suddenly becomes unattractive and a brief change is required.

From the point of view of certain owners, these diet-shifts are nothing but a nuisance, but if ever, for some dramatic reason, the cat found itself without its usual owner, they would stand it in good stead. For they would enable the cat to switch more easily to whatever new food regimen was forced upon it by altered circumstances.

There is a seeming contradiction in cat feeding that must be mentioned here. If one cat is always given a completely monotonous (but nutritionally complete) diet, day in and day out, always the same brand of canned cat food, it may eventually refuse to touch any other, new kind of food, no matter how tasty. If another cat is given a much more interesting and varied diet, with a different kind of canned food each day and many other titbits, then, paradoxically, it may refuse one of its old, favourite foods from time to time. At first glance this does not make sense. The explanation is that, given a totally unvarying diet over a long period of time, especially if it is from kittenhood right through into adult life, a cat's 'food variety mechanism' gets worn down and is finally switched off altogether. It develops what is called 'neophobia', or 'fear of the new'. Novel tastes and smells become threatening. New foods are rejected. Such cats can become a real problem if their rigid daily routine is upset – say by the death of an elderly owner. The other type of cat – one that is given a more excitingly varied diet – has its 'food variety mechanism' fully activated throughout its life and therefore becomes more demanding and fussy with food. In other words, given no food choice a cat gives up asking for variety; given variety it demands more.

Can a cat survive on a vegetarian diet?

No, it is quite impossible for a cat – any cat – to survive on a vegetarian or vegan diet. Given a meatless diet it will rapidly become ill and will then die a painful death. A cat is a carnivore and if it is to be kept as a pet it must be given a carnivorous diet.

Nutritional experts have been criticized in the past for expressing themselves so strongly on this point, but they are unrepentant. If adult human beings wish to impose upon themselves an inappropriate and inefficient diet, that is their own business. But if they impose such a diet on their pet cats, they should be prosecuted for cruelty to animals.

This statement will anger many well-meaning vegetarians and vegans, but they must face the biological facts. Cats and humans both evolved as meat-eaters – as predators – and until our biochemists have been able to produce synthetic meats, with the magic mixture of essential amino-acids, we are both trapped by our evolutionary past. This does not reflect a lack of sympathy with the ethical basis of vegetarianism, far from it. Few people are happy about the idea of an animal having to die so that either they or their pet can can feed, and might well be prepared to eat a synthetic steak if one could be produced – and to serve it up to their cat. However, until that stage is reached, all we can do is to ensure that the animals whose flesh we devour are given the best possible lifestyle and are then despatched as quickly and painlessly as possible. If we cannot face the idea of feeding animal products to our pets then we should switch from keeping cats to keeping canaries.

For those who require more specific evidence to convince them, there are three key facts. Firstly, cats need an amino-acid called taurine to prevent them from going blind. Without it the retinas of their eyes would rapidly deteriorate. Some animals can manufacture taurine from other sources, but the cat cannot do so. It can only obtain it by eating animal proteins. So without a meat diet a cat would soon lose its sight.

Secondly, cats must have animal fats in their diets because they are incapable of manufacturing essential fatty acids without them. Some other animals can manage to convert vegetable oils into these fatty acids, but cats lack this ability. Without animal fats to eat, cats would, among other serious problems, find it difficult to achieve reproduction, blood-clotting and new cell production.

Thirdly, unlike many other animals, cats are unable to obtain vitamin A from plant sources (such as carrots) and must rely instead for this crucial substance on animal foods such as liver, kidney or fish oils.

These facts alone underline the folly of recent attempts to convert cat owners to vegetarian regimes for their pets.

Why do cats drink dirty water?

A number of owners have noticed, to their dismay, that their feline pets seem to have a passion for drinking from puddles and pools of water in the garden. They do this despite the fact that on the kitchen floor there is an immaculately clean dish of pure tap water, and probably milk as well, awaiting them. For some reason they ignore these hygienic delights and go padding off to some stagnant puddle to lap up the filthy water there. Why do they do it?

All the best books on cat care insist that cats should always have access to fresh, clean water and that the water should be changed regularly. They also tell their readers that the dish itself must be cleaned repeatedly to avoid any infection or contamination. But they overlook two problems. Fresh tap water is usually heavily treated with chemicals and often chlorinated strongly enough actually to have a chemical smell. The cat's sensitive nose cannot stand this. Worse still, the dish has probably been cleaned out with some form of modern detergent. This is bad enough on food dishes, but with those there is at least the powerful odour of the fish or meat to smother the distasteful detergent smell. With drinking dishes, however, the smell of the detergent is simply added to the already unpleasant odour of the treated water, with the result that the cat will only drink from its official dish if it has no alternative. The stale water in the puddles and pools outside is much more attractive. It may be full of microbes and rotting vegetation, but these are natural and organic and only give it an attractive flavour.

Veterinary authors issue dire warnings about the risk of 'transmission of disease' resulting from permitting your cat to drink from ponds and puddles, begging the question of how so many wild animals manage to remain perfectly healthy. In reality, the risk is really rather slight, though even this can be eliminated by taking more trouble to rinse off all the detergent from the cat's dishes. Because cats are many times more sensitive to detergent contamination than we humans are, much more rinsing than usual is required. Also, the fresh tap water should be allowed to stand for some time before being offered to the cat, to allow the chemicals to dissipate. Then, perhaps, the finicky felines will deign to dip their tongues into the clean water you offer them.

Also on the subject of drinking, a cat should never be given milk alone in place of water. If milk is offered, it should be given alongside water, so that the animal has a choice. Many adult cats, contrary to popular opinion, actively dislike milk, and it is not necessary for them. For some, especially Siamese cats, it can cause gastric upsets, and if milk is given without alternative water, such cats are liable to suffer from diarrhoea.

What smells actively repel cats?

The chemical smells of modern tap water may stop a cat drinking from its bowl, but they are not strong enough to drive the animal back physically from the corner of the kitchen floor where the bowl is placed. Odours offensive enough to put a cat into full retreat are rare. This creates a problem for people who are looking for something that cats dislike, to use as a repellent. When a pet cat has started scratching the fabric of a valuable chair, for example, or has begun to make messes on an expensive carpet, it would be helpful to be able to sprinkle or smear some hated odour there to keep the animal away. But what can be used?

Searching back through the long history of feline deterrents, there appear to have been only three smelly substances that have achieved a measure of success. The first is the oil of the crushed leaves of a small aromatic bush called 'rue'. As long ago as the first century A.D., the Roman author Pliny, in his monumental Natural History, suggested that placing branches of this shrub around an object would keep cats away from it. This advice was still being offered 1,200 years later, in the Middle Ages, when an expert on herb gardens wrote, 'Behind the turf plot let there be a great diversity of medicinal and aromatic herbs, among which Rue should be mingled in many places for its beauty and greenness, and its bitterness will drive away poisonous animals from the garden.' Some modern gardeners report that handling the leaves of this plant can cause a blistering rash on sensitive skin, so it must obviously be treated with respect, but there is a good chance that oil of rue would prove to be a successful repellent for most misbehaving cats. For some reason this ancient piece of folk-wisdom seems to have been largely forgotten, but it might be worth reviving it in cases where ordinary measures have failed.

A second and perhaps easier suggestion is the use of onions. By rubbing a raw onion over the area to be protected, a cat can usually be deterred, and the smell, although unpleasant for humans at first, soon goes unnoticed. Most cats, however, continue to find it distasteful long after the human occupants of the rooms have forgotten about it.

The most effective deterrent, however, is that simple household substance, vinegar. Cats loathe it. The acid fragrance upsets their delicate nasal passages and they avoid anything smeared in it for long periods of time. Short of buying special, commercially prepared cat-repellent sprays from a local pet shop, it is the best weapon available.

It must be added, though, that cats are stubborn animals and will often consider such chemical warfare as a kind of challenge. Their first reaction will be to shift the location of their activities. If this fails, after a while they may manage to overcome their distaste for a particular substance and then it is necessary to change one's tactics. Ultimately, the best solution is to try and defeat the cat's damaging ways by using understanding and intelligence rather than foul-smelling chemicals. If the behaviour behind the unwanted feline activity can be analyzed, it may be possible to find a psychological solution which, in the long run, will always be more successful.

Note:

Since completing this book I have been able to obtain a cutting of *rue* and test its effect on my own cat. Placed on the carpet, it attracted her and she sat sniffing it closely. But when I rubbed the leaves between my fingers and offered her my fingertips to sniff, her reaction was dramatic. She brought her nose up to my hand, then leapt backwards, opened her mouth and tried to vomit. After that she stalked off and refused to come near me. I washed my hands and tried to make my peace with her, but when I went to stroke her she hissed at me. Ten minutes later, she miaowed if I approached her and it took her several hours to forgive me and to stop treating me like a walking cat repellent.

Why do some cats foul the house?

Some owners are distressed to discover that, after months or years of 'clean' behaviour, their pet cats start to leave messes around the house. In the past such animals have been models of cleanliness, always asking to go outside before defecating, or confining themselves to a modern litter tray. Now suddenly, for no apparent reason, they become careless and leave their faeces on the carpet. If there is no obvious explanation for this loss of restraint, what is the hidden one?

The first possibility is that the cat in question is ill or senile and its whole behaviour routine is starting to collapse. In such cases a vet is needed urgently. But many cats who foul the house are clearly perfectly healthy, at least physically. So what is their mental state, that causes them to behave in this very unfeline-like way?

One factor that is important could be classified as 'territorial disruption'. Some people find that the trouble begins when they have the builders in and the house undergoes some kind of dramatic redesigning. Cats hate this and, if a new wing has been added to the home for example, will defecate on the floor of the new area, almost as a comment on how they feel about the upheaval. One owner found that his cat did this only on the floor of a new extension he had built on to the side of his house. The rest of the dwelling was treated with as much respect as before, but the new room was − as far as the cat was concerned − still part of the 'outside' and was treated accordingly.

A second factor is 'social disruption'. If a new kitten is brought into the home the old cat may feel slighted by all the attention the newcomer is receiving. It will feel the need to express its dominance and will do this in the manner of a 'top cat'. This means leaving faeces in a prominent place, rather than covering them up in the litter tray. Most people still imagine that all cats cover their droppings, but this is not so. Only friendly or subordinate cats cover them up. Aggressively dominant, wild-living cats leave them openly in conspicuous places as 'odour threats'. In an undisturbed home, all domestic cats see themselves as subordinates of their human owners, so under normal circumstances all domestic cats use litter trays or bury their faeces in the garden. But if they suddenly have the urge to express their senior status in relation to a new pet in the home they may revert to the age-old manner of doing this, much to the distress of their well-meaning owners, who probably bought the new kitten as a special companion for the older cat.

A third possibility, and perhaps the most likely explanation, is that the cat's litter tray leaves something to be desired. Cats hate to bury their faeces in a place where they have recently done so. In the garden you will see them nosing around trying to find a new place to dig a hole. In the litter tray they do the same thing, but if it has been used several times without being properly cleaned out this becomes impossible and the cat will then prefer to defecate elsewhere, even if it has to go through the motions of covering its dung with imaginary earth after it has deposited it on a wooden floor or a carpet. The secret in such cases is to increase the rate of emptying and cleaning the litter tray.

A final factor has to do with the position of the litter tray. Cats hate to defecate where they eat and some people place the litter tray too near the animal's food dish. Or they place it in a busy part of the house, near the back door, where people are always walking past. Cats feel vulnerable when they are defecating and do not like to have anyone near them at that time. So if a litter tray is in too public a place, this too may drive them elsewhere.

If the trouble has started and does not look like stopping, the best solution is to provide an immaculately clean tray of fresh litter, place it in a quiet corner, and then shut the animal up in that particular room, releasing it only when it has used the tray in the approved manner. In this way it is possible to re-start the routine that was enjoyed previously, although it may take some days of patience to break the new habit.

What is poisonous to cats?

Apart from the obvious poisons, cats are susceptible to a number of substances they may encounter in their daily lives. Nearly all of these are modern chemicals we have thoughtlessly introduced into our cats' environment to help us in various ways. In our urge to cleanse and control our world we have, for cats, often unwittingly polluted it.

The worst offenders are the disinfectants and pesticides. We may need them, but we should also spare a thought for our cats when using them, or sooner or later our pet animals will suffer. This applies both inside the house and outside, in the garden and on farmlands. Wild animals are not alone in suffering from some of the technological advances of modern agriculture.

One of the greatest hazards for today's free-roaming feline is the use of rodent poisons. Many people have employed a variety of mouse and rat poisons without stopping to think that the initial effect of such toxins is to slow down the victim which then becomes an easy target for a hunting cat. In other words, the dying mouse is the one most likely to end up in a cat's stomach. Inside the mouse's body, of course, the poison that made it so easy to catch is still present and can cause serious damage to the unfortunate cat. After eating its mouse, the cat may start to vomit, froth at the mouth and stagger about in a confused condition. Its heart beat may speed up or become weak, its breathing heavy and laboured, and it may eventually go into convulsions or start bleeding. If the rodent it ate had been heavily dosed, the cat may die. This is a case of adding injury to insult – it was originally the cat's job to kill the mice and the rodent-poisoners who usurped its role are not content merely with making it obsolete, but are also assaulting it physically in this underhand, prey-concealed way.

Another danger comes from domestic powders and sprays that are employed excessively – on the lawn for example. Cats that lie down on grass soaked in weed-killer and then fastidiously lick their fur clean will ingest this type of poison with alarming ease. Indoors, the various chemical insect-killers, disinfectants and furniture-cleaning sprays may also contaminate the pet cat's fur as the animal lies on the floor or on some other surface. Again it is the cat's obsessive cleanliness, driving it to groom its fur with its tongue, that accidentally transports these 'helpful' chemicals into its system. Small traces may not hurt, but in households where modern hygiene has become a fanatical pursuit, the unhappy pet is at some risk.

One of the mistakes we make is to imagine that if something is harmless or beneficial to us it must automatically be so to cats. Certain pain-killers we use – even something as mild and commonplace as aspirin – can be damaging to the cat. If we humanize the cat to the extent where we start to give it human medication, we may be hurting it when we are trying to be kind. If a cat is sick we should always take veterinary advice.

Sometimes, at Christmas or a special party, someone decides it would be fun to give the household cat a 'treat' by lacing its milk with alcohol. Most cats will refuse to join in such celebrations, but those that do will quickly suffer for it. Our human digestive system has a struggle with such things as alcohol, but we are resilient and are rather good at detoxifying the many dubious substances that we inflict on our long-suffering internal organs. The digestive system of the cat is less successful in this respect and often fails to break down the dangerous elements in ingested substances to make them harmless. Just as they cannot cope with the nutritional inferiority of a vegetarian diet, so they find it hard to deal with even a moderate dose of alcohol and may start to vomit, collapse or even go into a coma. Sobriety suits the domestic cat.

Finally there is one ancient, natural poison that can plague an inexperienced feline. The young adult cat, venturing into the garden in the spring, is excited to discover a prey that is mysteriously easy to catch. The common toad hops clumsily along and is incapable of making a sudden dart for cover. The cat is transfixed by this appealing sight and pounces, sinking its teeth into the prey. A moment later, the cat is in acute distress. Its mouth is turning red and swelling up. It starts to retch and dribble. Another over-eager cat has discovered one of the basic truths of garden life: never try to kill a toad.

The humble toad, so slow and cumbersome that it looks like

easy pickings for any predatory mammal or bird, has survived for millions of years because it has managed to evolve a particularly virulent poison called *bufotalin*. This is contained in the large warts that cover the upper surface of the toad's skin. These warts are no danger to a human being because they only exude their poisonous fluid if the toad is being injured. If the animal is bitten hard by a cat, or by some other unwary predator, the warts ooze poison into the attacker's clasping jaws. The toad is quickly dropped and escapes – with no more than a few minor punctures if it is lucky. It is significant that the two largest warts are positioned on either side of the top of its thick neck – precisely the place where a cat likes to sink its fangs when making its killing bite. In fact, these two warts are so enlarged that they look like long swellings behind the animal's eyes, covered with pores through which the poison seeps. Bearing in mind that it only takes 20 milligrams of this poison to kill a dog, and that a cat is equally susceptible, it is clear that here we have a serious threat to an incautious feline. Perhaps this is the origin of the old expression 'curiosity killed the cat'? Fortunately most pet cats, if they do encounter a toad, quickly learn that it tastes bad and, after one preliminary nip, rapidly drop the squirming amphibian and never make the same mistake again. Only the really savage hunter, who sinks his fangs deep into the toad's neck at its very first contact, will suffer a major trauma or death.

A final word of warning. Anti-freeze tastes sweet and cats like the flavour of it. If a pet cat has access to the garage where someone has been filling the car's radiator system with anti-freeze at the onset of winter, the animal may see a small puddle on the garage floor, where some has spilled. If it laps up a little of this, the ethylene glycol may cause irreversible kidney damage. The cat may even fall into a deep coma. The problem is that the pool of liquid usually forms underneath the car, where it is both inconspicuous and difficult to get at, so the chances are that it will not be mopped up. Unfortunately the space beneath a car is much more accessible to a cat's small body and the damage is easily done. Many times when a much-loved pet falls sick we think first of diseases and infections, when the real cause is simple chemical poisoning of a completely accidental nature.

Why do some cats become wool-suckers?

Some cat owners notice that their cats become wool-suckers at a certain age and they worry about this apparently abnormal behaviour. They are right to do so, because it can lead to serious problems if it persists. Strands of wool are loosened by the prolonged sucking and may be swallowed, leading eventually to a blockage of the cat's intestines, requiring surgery. Why do they do it?

The clue is in the way they perform the sucking action. They find some woollen garment or other soft furnishing in the house and then settle down on it in a contented fashion. Pressing the mouth to it, they start to suck or chew it rhythmically while treading alternately with their front feet. While doing this they appear to be lost in pleasure and increasingly unaware of the world around them. Clearly there is a huge reward for them in performing these seemingly useless actions and, were it not for the risk of ingesting the wool fragments, there would be no harm in it.

The reason for the attraction of the wool is not hard to find. The actions directed towards the cloth are identical with those performed by a tiny kitten when feeding at its mother's nipple. The trampling movements are intended to stimulate her milk flow and when these are done by the wool-sucking cat they reveal that it is treating the piece of woollen material as a surrogate mother. In other words wool-sucking is the act of feeding at a 'ghost-nipple' and is the feline equivalent of thumb-sucking in human babies (or pipe-sucking in elderly human males).

Wool-sucking seems to be most common among young cats that have been orphaned or have for some other reason been deprived of the maternal nipple too soon. It usually starts shortly after the animals have been weaned and in most instances it only persists for a few months. But for some cats – especially Siamese – it continues for a lifetime and is extremely difficult to eradicate.

The special attraction of wool is that the presence of lanolin acts as a powerful unconscious reminder of the mother's belly. Sucking the wool and making it damp enhances the lanolin odour, and this keeps the cats contented and fully absorbed in their sucking and chewing.

If there is no wool available to them, cats with an urge to re-create the pleasures of sucking at the maternal nipple have been known to suck their own fur, sometimes their feet and sometimes the tips of their tails; or they occasionally develop a fixation on their owner's hair and make repeated attempts to suck on that, if they are given half a chance.

Some authorities have suggested a change in diet for such cats, but there seems little logic in this unless the new diet helps to reduce boredom. An empty lifestyle does seem to increase the chances of wool-sucking, and probably the best cure for it would be to make the cat's way of life more surprising and complex. More drastic cures, such as providing woollen garments covered in some noxious chemical substance, do not really cure the cat's fixation. All that happens is that the animal waits until the treated garments are discarded and then homes in on some other, more suitable surface. The wool-sucking then starts up once again, unabated, and it is impossible to keep up a permanent 'treatment' of all potential woollen materials. Sooner or later the cat will win and wear down its owner's resolve. The only true solution is somehow to alter the cat's mental state and rid it of the monotony or stress that drives it to perform the 'pseudo-infantile' actions.

Why does a cat sometimes bite the hand that strokes it?

Some cats are completely docile and allow as much petting and stroking as their human companions wish to lavish upon them. Others, if they have had enough attention, will simply start to struggle and then leap down or move away. But there is another type of cat – more common than most people suppose – that has a more violent reaction to being over-petted. Described by one author as the Jekyll and Hyde Cat, this animal suddenly lashes out and attacks its friendly owner's hand. The assault is so unexpected and apparently unjustified that it leaves the owner not only bleeding but also deeply perplexed.

Before explaining the cause of this reaction, it helps to observe precisely what happens. First the owner starts to stroke the cat, tickle its ear, or gently rub its head. The cat responds lovingly, totally relaxed and probably purring. Then, after a while, it stiffens imperceptibly and, often unnoticed by the stroker, its ears start to rotate so that their backs face forward. This is the key danger signal. At the same moment the pupils may dilate. Then, so fast that the movements are almost impossible to analyze, the cat lashes out with its claws extended, raking the skin of the hand in front of it. At the same time it may make a sudden, savage bite with its canines. Then in a flash it dashes away as if fleeing in panic.

Essentially this is the behaviour of a cat that feels itself severely threatened and strikes out to protect itself. Having done this and expecting immediate reprisals, it then runs for cover. But why does it suddenly feel threatened by the contact of its peaceful owner? There appear to be two possible explanations. The first has to do with the individual animal's past history. It often happens that a particular cat finds itself betrayed by a friendly human hand. The fingers move gently in and start to tickle it or rub its face and then, without warning, grab it and pick it up. This is the strategy employed by strangers who are fearful of the cat's claws and have to find some way of picking it up without being attacked. A vet who wishes to examine a cat may approach it in this way before, for instance, holding it down to give it an injection. Cats have long memories, especially where a nasty shock is concerned, and may remember a bad experience of this kind for years afterwards. This creates a conflict for them because, although they want to be stroked and petted like any other domestic cat, they are deeply suspicious of the hand that does the petting, fearing that at any moment it may grab them and hold them down. At the start of the contact the need to be stroked is so strong that it suppresses their fear. As the seconds tick by, however, and this need becomes increasingly satisfied, the fear of being grabbed starts to well up inside them. Suddenly it takes over – uncontrollably, they lash out and then flee in panic, their ancient memory switching them from Jekyll to Hyde.

For cats without this unpleasant memory there is less chance that they will bite the hand that strokes them, but it can still happen occasionally. To understand this it is necessary to consider the meaning of the stroking and petting, not from our point of view but from the cat's.

Adult cats occasionally groom one another, but the most common form of social grooming is the licking of kittens by their mother. The kittens tolerate a certain amount of this before deciding that enough is enough. To the adult pet cat living with human companions, its owner's hand is a symbolic 'mother's tongue' tugging at or smoothing its fur. When it has had enough 'cleaning' its mood changes and the hand ceases to fill the role of a maternal tongue. Without changing its movements, it now becomes the 'giant paw' of a huge cat – in this new role it is suddenly threatening and the animal responds appropriately with a defensive reaction.

Is it cruel to have a cat de-clawed?

Yes, it is. To remove a cat's claws is far worse than to deprive cat owners of their finger-nails. This is because the claws have so many important functions in the life of a cat. A de-clawed cat is a maimed cat and anyone considering having the operation done to their pet should think again.

Consider the facts. To begin with, it is important that every cat should keep itself well groomed. A smooth, clean coat of fur is essential for a cat's well-being. It is vital for temperature control, for cleanliness, for waterproofing and for controlling the scent-signalling of the feline body. As a result, cats spend a great deal of time every day dealing with their toilet, and in addition to the typical licking movements they perform repeated scratchings. These scratching actions are a crucial part of the cleaning routine, getting rid of skin irritations, dislodging dead hairs and combing out tangles in the fur. Without claws it is impossible for any cat to scratch itself efficiently and the whole grooming pattern suffers as a result. Even if human owners help out with brush and comb, there is no way they can replace the sensitivity of the natural scratching response of their pet. Any people who have ever suffered from itches that they cannot scratch will sympathize with the dilemma of the de-clawed cat.

It has been argued that a de-clawed cat can learn to use its teeth more when grooming. It is true that cats often nibble an irritation, rather than scratch it, but unfortunately some of the most urgent scratching requirements are in the region of the head, mouth, neck and especially the ears. Teeth are useless here and these important parts of the body cannot be kept in perfect condition with only clawless feet to groom them.

A second problem faces the de-clawed cat, when it tries to climb. Climbing is second nature to all small felines and it is virtually impossible for a cat to switch off its urge to climb, even if it is punished for doing so. And punished it certainly will be if it attempts to climb after having its claws removed, for it will no longer have any grip in its feet. Out of doors, if it is being chased by a rival cat, a dog, or some human enemy, it will try, as always, to scamper up a wall or a tree, using its non-existent claws to cling to the surfaces as it leaps upwards. To its horror it will find itself slipping and sliding, tumbling down at the mercy of its foes. When it turns to face them it will be at an even greater disadvantage because, when it strikes out at them with its paws, it will find itself robbed of its defensive weapons and unable to protect itself. Often, it is only the sharpness of the pain caused by the stiletto-pointed claws that stands between life and death for a cornered cat.

In less dramatic contexts, for de-clawed cats kept indoors (and robbed of all outdoor pleasures), even the simple act of climbing up on to a chair or a window-ledge may prove hazardous. Without the pinpoint contact of the tips of the claws, the animals may find themselves slipping and crashing to the ground. The expression of confusion observed on the faces of such cats as they pick themselves up is in itself sufficient to turn any cat-lover against the idea of claw-removal.

In addition to destroying the animal's ability to groom, climb, defend itself against rivals and protect itself from enemies, the operation of de-clawing also eliminates the cat's ability to hunt. This may not be important for a well-fed family pet, but if ever such a cat were to find itself lost or homeless it would rapidly die of starvation. The vital grab at a mouse with sharp claws extended would become a useless gesture.

In short, a de-clawed cat is a crippled, mutilated cat and no excuse can justify the operation. Despite this, many pet cats are carried off to the vet by exasperated owners for this type of 'convenience surgery'. The operation, although nearly always refused by vets in Britain, has become so common in certain countries that it even has an official name. It is called *onyxectomy*. Using an old Greek name for it somehow makes it seem more respectable. The literal translation of onyxectomy, however, is simply 'nail-cutting-out' and that is what vets are doing, even though they may not like to be reminded of the fact when they record their day's work.

It has been argued by some cat experts that any vet performing this convenience operation should be prosecuted for cruelty to animals, but this is unfair to them. They may well be faced with owners who demand that the operation be done, with the only alternative that their pet cat be destroyed. Given such a choice, and a perfectly healthy cat, it is hard to blame the vet for selecting the lesser of two evils. If there is any prosecution, it should be of the owner rather than the vet.

The reason for the popularity of the de-clawing operation in recent years has been the concern of (usually wealthy) owners for their soft furnishings. Valuable chair fabrics, curtains, cushions and other materials are often found scratched, torn and tattered as a result of the family cat's claw-sharpening activities around the house. This is especially troublesome in urban homes, where the animals have little access to wooden posts or trees. And the addition of commercially manufactured 'scratching-posts' to the indoor furniture rarely seems to solve the problem. There are only three solutions: the owners can decide that the pleasure of having a cat in the home is greater than the distress of living with scratched furniture, or some kind of covering that cats hate to scratch has to be put over the sides of the furniture, or the cats have to be trained not to strop the furniture with their claws. This last alternative is a possibility, but it is by no means easy. Shouting at cats or hitting them has little effect. It is best to take a leaf out of the mother cat's book. When she wants to control her kittens, she growls at them. They learn this signal and soon respond to it. Growling like a mother cat may make a cat owner feel ridiculous, but if it helps to restrain a cat from tearing at a valuable chair, it is well worth a try.

Finally, a word of praise for the organizers of pedigree cat shows. All too often they are accused of exploiting cats to satisfy the competitive urges of the exhibitors, and it might be imagined that they would favour the de-clawing operation to facilitate the handling of cats when they are being judged at shows. Nothing could be further from the truth. Despite many a scratched hand, the official ruling is that any pedigree cat found to have had its claws removed is automatically and unconditionally disqualified from competing. Supporting this attitude are new moves in the veterinary world to outlaw totally the operation for any cats, both pedigree and moggie. Britain is leading the way in this and it is hoped that other countries will soon follow suit.

Why do cats sulk?

A scolded cat often turns its back on its owners and haughtily refuses to look at them. One owner describes this 'cold shoulder treatment' in the following words: 'He turns his back, sits down neatly and deliberately, and won't answer if we call his name as he usually does, though he sometimes puts one ear back.' This behaviour, observed by many owners when their pets have been chastised or corrected in some way, is usually referred to as a dignified sulk. But what is the cat really doing?

The answer is not that it is demonstrating 'wounded pride', as its owners believe, but instead is revealing its social inferiority. Its haughtiness is apparent, not real. This is hard for some owners to accept, because they have such respect for their feline companions. But they overlook the fact that, to the cat, they are huge and therefore psychologically overwhelming. When a cat misbehaves and its owner reacts crossly, the cat feels threatened. An owner's anger at some feline misdeed usually involves harsh tones and fixed staring. Staring is very intimidating to a cat and its natural response is to avoid the hostile image of the staring eyes. This it does by turning away in a deliberate manner and refusing to look again at the glowering face. Hence the apparent haughtiness of the 'turn-my-back-on-you' posture.

This action is called 'cut-off' because it cuts off the input – the hostile face looming over it. It has a double effect: it reduces the fear in the cat itself and enables it to stay where it is, rather than move off into the distance; it also prevents any counter-staring by the cat, which would spell defiance and possibly provoke further hostility.

The importance of this 'anti-stare' in feline social life is evident whenever two cats are involved in a status battle. The dominant cat always keeps a fixed stare directed towards its rival. The subordinate cat, if it wants to hold its ground, deliberately looks right away from its enemy and makes abso-

47

lutely sure that its gaze never goes anywhere near the eyes of the glaring overlord. In the human context, this threat-stare has become a regular ritual of major boxing matches. When the referee talks to the two boxers just before the first round, each fighter stares closely and directly into the opponent's eyes. Neither dares to look away for an instant, in case this is read as a sign of weakness. For the 'sulking' cat, this sign of weakness is being deliberately displayed as a response to its owner's threats.

Any people who doubt this can carry out a simple test devised by the great cat authority, Paul Leyhausen, the next time they visit a zoo. Leyhausen proved the power of the direct stare by standing in front of a tiger's cage and hiding his eyes. He did this by bringing a camera up to his face, through which he could nevertheless still see the tiger's actions. The animal crouched ready for an attack and then dashed across its cage floor towards the spot where Leyhausen was standing. As it came near he quickly lowered the camera and directed a wide-eyed stare, straight at the big cat. It skidded to a halt immediately and rapidly looked away, avoiding the man's gaze. As soon as he covered his eyes with his camera again, another attack was launched. Again he froze it with a quick stare, and was able to repeat this process time and again.

Apart from the fact that this provides a valuable lesson for anyone unexpectedly encountering a big cat at close quarters, it explains the way in which lion-tamers at a circus manage to dominate their animal companions. A fixed stare from the trainer and they look away, remaining placidly ('sulkily') in their place.

The stare-threat phenomenon also explains another oddity of feline behaviour. Some observers have noticed that domestic cats, when hunting small birds in the garden, appear to be amazingly intelligent in one particular respect. If the bird's head disappears behind some small obstruction, the cat can be seen to rush forward and pounce, as though it knows that at that moment the bird cannot see its rapid advance. For the cat to reason this out would require considerable mental agility, but there is of course a simpler explanation. As long as the bird's eye is visible, it is automatically giving the cat a 'stare' that inhibits its attacking lunge. Once the eye is accidentally hidden behind some obstruction, the stare is switched off and the cat can attack. Studies of big cats stalking prey have revealed a similar interaction. If the prey looks up and stares straight at the lion or tiger, the big cat looks sheepishly away as if suddenly indifferent to the whole business of predation. So for any prey with the courage to hold its ground and out-stare a hunting lion, there is some considerable advantage to be gained . . . unless of course there is another lion coming up from behind . . .

Why do cats prefer to die alone?

Cat owners are sometimes distressed by the fact that their favourite and much-loved cat leaves them shortly before it dies. After years of being cared for and protected in a human family, the elderly feline disappears one day and is then found dead in a corner of the garden shed next door, or in some even more secretive place. The owners feel spurned, wondering why their cat has not come to them for help when it feels seriously ill. To abandon them at such a moment implies that they did not, after all, mean so much to the animal – they were not a 'safe haven' in quite the way they had pictured themselves. But they do themselves an injustice.

This 'dying alone' is not a new phenomenon. An oriental author, writing as long ago as 1708, records that one of the cat's unique features is that 'it perishes in a place quite out of human sight, as if it wills not to let man see its dying look, which is unusually ugly'. Much later, a mere half century ago, the author Alan Devoe makes a similar comment: 'One day, often with no forewarning whatever, he is gone from the house and never returns. He has felt the presaging shadow of death, and he goes to meet it in the old unchanging way of the wild – alone. A cat does not want to die with the smell of humanity in his nostrils and the noise of humanity in his delicate peaked ears. Unless death strikes very quickly and suddenly, he creeps away to where it is proper that a proud wild beast should die – not on one of man's rags or cushions, but in a lonely quiet place, with his muzzle pressed against the cold earth.'

The motives described by these authors are little more than romantic inventions, but the fact that the dying cat's actions have been recorded in this way by very different writers is of some interest. Clearly we are dealing here with a feline phenomenon that is not isolated and accidental, but more a regular, typical feature of cat behaviour. If only a few cases were known, they could easily be the result of an animal just happening to die when in a remote spot. A human being who

50

suffers a fatal heart attack when out walking in a wood would not have been setting out to 'die alone'. But with cats it seems to be too common to be explained in this way.

To understand the behaviour it is essential to consider the question of how a cat faces death. We humans all know we are going to die one day and we act accordingly. A cat has no concept of its own death and so it cannot anticipate it, no matter how ill it feels. What falling ill means to a cat, or any other animal, is that something unpleasant is threatening it. If it feels pain, it considers itself to be under attack. It is difficult for it to distinguish between one sort of pain and another, when trying to work out what is going wrong. If the pain becomes acute, the cat knows that it is in great danger. If it cannot see the source of the danger, it cannot turn to face it and lash out in defence – there is nothing there at which to lash out. This leaves only two alternative strategies: to flee or to hide. If the pain comes on when the cat is out patrolling its territory, its natural reaction will be to attempt to hide from the 'attacker'. If the cat sees a shed nearby, or some other hiding place, it will make for this and then stay concealed, alone, waiting for the threat to pass, for the pain to ease. It dare not come out, in case the source of the pain is waiting for it, and so it remains there, dying alone and in private. Despite the earlier authors' comments on the matter, at the moment of death the cat is not thinking of its human owners' feelings, but simply about how it can protect itself from the terrifying, unseen danger that is causing it so much pain.

If we feel sorry for the dying cat that cannot understand what is happening to it, we should remember that it has one enormous advantage over us: it has no fear of death, which is something we humans must all carry with us throughout our long lives.

Why do cats suddenly make mad dashes around the house?

Cat owners often notice that their pet will suddenly and for no apparent reason make a headlong dash through the house. Moving at top speed, the animal positively flings itself along and then, just as suddenly, comes to rest as though nothing strange has occurred. When this behaviour is seen for the first time, the owners may become seriously concerned, imagining that the cat is having some kind of fit or seizure. Unaware of how common this outburst of activity really is among house-bound cats, they interpret it as some sort of abnormality and may even call in the vet to examine the animal. But their fears are groundless. There is nothing unusual about the feline 'mad dash'. Almost all cats do it and there is a simple explanation.

The mad dash is what is called a 'vacuum' activity. Cats kept indoors a great deal, with every whim catered to and with plenty of food always available, eventually come to suffer from a special kind of deprivation. They lack the opportunity to express their inborn urges to hunt and to flee from danger. There is no prey to catch and no predators or rivals from which to escape. Day after day, the finely-tuned responses that all felines possess – to make a sudden rush towards an unsuspecting mouse, or to make a headlong flight from approaching danger – are thwarted by the peace and luxurious calm of the home in which they live. They reach a point where even the smallest stimulus will trigger off a massive reaction. The pent-up energy overflows and a mad dash is on.

Proof that these outbursts are overflow or vacuum activities rather than pathological fits can be found by comparing the indoor behaviour of hard-living rural cats, with that of lap-of-luxury town cats. The working cats spend much of their time outside chasing birds and rodents, or challenging rival cats, and are wonderfully relaxed when they do, at last, come indoors for a saucer of milk or a snooze by the fire. Their main preoccupation is licking and grooming themselves and their

52

most vigorous activity is likely to be the languorous stretching of tired limbs. The pampered town cat, by contrast, is often seen to be prowling around the house like a caged tiger. Even if it does go outside, there is little to hunt on the manicured lawns, and no serious threat from feline neighbours. So, when it returns for yet another pre-killed dish of food, it may find itself in a listless, frustrated mood. After resting for a while, it suddenly gets up, looks around and then sets off on one of its mad dashes. In this way it is able to release some of its hunting or fleeing energy and to feel more relaxed again.

Some owners report that their cats are liable to do this immediately after using the litter box. Others see it occurring at exactly the same time each day, but with no obvious connection with any other activity. Still others observe that it usually starts with a 'trigger action' of some sort. Such actions are usually in the form of a mock attack from a human friend, the presence of some kind of 'ghost prey', or some sharp, sudden sound or movement. The cats use these triggers as an 'excuse', so to speak, to release the frustrated response. Sometimes they even seem to provoke the trigger actions deliberately. A cat may approach its human owner and purposely make a nuisance of itself in a way that it has learnt will cause anger. When the owner shouts at the cat, instead of simply stopping as it usually does, the cat will massively over-react with one of its mad-panic rushes. The response is out of all proportion to the stimulus, and this is what makes it special, distinguishing it from occasions where a cat merely withdraws after being scolded.

Why are cats attracted to people who dislike them?

If a cat enters a room where several people are talking, it is very likely to make for the one person there who has an abnormal fear of felines. To that individual's horrified disbelief, the animal then proceeds to rub around his or her legs and may even jump up on the person's lap. Why is the cat so perverse?

To some people, this is a confirmation of the old idea that there is something inherently wicked in the feline personality, and that the animal deliberately selects someone with a cat phobia and then sets out to cause them embarrassment. But this kind of superstitious romanticizing is superfluous. There is a much simpler explanation of the animal's behaviour.

When the cat enters the room and looks around, it notices that several people are staring at it. They are the cat-lovers, gazing at the cat because they like it. But, in feline terms, to be stared at is to be mildly threatened. Children are sometimes told 'it is rude to stare', but cat-lovers often forget this rule when they are looking at an approaching feline. Instead of a glance, which is always acceptable, they keep staring at the animal in a way that makes it feel uncomfortable. The only person there not doing this is the cat-hater, who looks away and keeps very still, trying to be ignored by the feared animal. But such behaviour has precisely the opposite effect. For the cat, in search of a friendly lap on which to sit, makes a bee-line for this ideal companion, who is *not* moving around, *not* waving hands about, *not* making shrill remarks and, above all, *not* staring. The cat is thus showing its appreciation of the non-intimidating body-language.

The secret for any cat-phobic individuals who want to keep their distance is to lean towards a cat, stare fixedly at it with wide-open eyes and make agitated hand movements, asking the cat in strident tones to come and sit on their laps. This will have exactly the opposite effect and they will then be able to relax without appearing to have insulted a host's favourite pet.

Why do some cats hate men?

Some owners notice that their cats love human females and hate or fear human males. Why do they make this distinction?

There are two factors at work here. One concerns the tonality of the human voice. The female voice, being much higher pitched, is closer in quality to that of the cat, which makes it more appealing. But this is not sufficient to explain the behaviour of some felines which will run and hide as soon as they hear a man approaching. In such cases it usually means that a man has, at some time in the past, hurt the cat in question. Cats have long memories and if they have suffered pain at male hands they may hate all males for months afterwards, sometimes literally for years.

This suggests that men are more cruel than women towards cats, but such an interpretation assumes that cats can distinguish between deliberate cruelty and pain inflicted for the animals' own good. The problem is that the majority of vets are men and cats often take a very long time to forget the helpful attentions they receive at their local animal clinics. The vet is only trying to assist the cat, but there is no way that the animal can associate the injection, or the forcible administration of a medicine, with its feeling healthier later on. All it knows is that when a human male came close to it, it was restrained and then something painful happened. So the next time a male voice, or a male footfall (for cats can quickly associate the heavy male tread with the deeper male voice), or the scent of a human male (for cats can also associate human odours with human genders) is detected, the cat thinks that trouble is on its way again, and beats a rapid retreat.

One particular cat, that was originally very friendly towards both men and women, demonstrated this extremely clearly. It was a stray that came to beg for food in the garden of a town house. When fed, it was happy to rub up against the legs of its new human friends, of either sex. Then someone offered to adopt the cat and the local vet was called in to give the animal a clean bill of health before it was moved to its new, permanent home. Cornered in a garden shed, the frightened cat was caught by the vet and given protective injections. It was then boxed up and taken to meet its new owner, an elderly woman living alone. The cat gradually made friends with her and became extremely loving, sleeping on her bed and following her everywhere, rubbing against her and jumping up on her lap. From a starving stray it was transformed into a contented house cat. But the memory of being caught and injected never faded, and even a year later the cat would still rush upstairs and hide beneath the bed if ever a man visited the house. In its mind it was convinced that the vet had returned to hurt it again. No amount of male kindness or pleading could reduce its fear. Visiting women, on the other hand, were always welcome and were treated to leg-rubbing and purring with as much friendship as was shown to its new owner. Its distinction between human males and human females was almost complete. There was only one exception, a very elderly male who sat quietly and hardly moved. Somehow the cat was capable of 'separating' in its mind this elderly man from the image of the much younger vet. It must be one of the major frustrations of being a veterinary surgeon that you can never convince your patients that you are on their side and are working tirelessly to save them and help them back to full health.

People who, with great kindness, acquire a rescued cat from an animal sanctuary, should be prepared for unusual reactions of this kind. They must never blame themselves for what happens, if the cat reacts fearfully to certain individuals or certain specific conditions. In such cases the animal is living in its past, a past about which the new owner knows little or nothing. Early traumas come back to haunt such cats and force them to behave in strange ways. Much patience is needed, but when eventually the cat does accept its new home, it will probably become the most loving and affectionate of all feline pets. It may even become over-affectionate, refusing to leave its rescuer alone, but this is simply a measure of its inner anxiety concerning the possibility that it may be betrayed once again. It is sometimes hard for cats to understand people and, like elephants, they never forget a shock encounter.

Why do some cats like to take walks with their owners?

Some cat manuals solemnly instruct their readers in how to take their pet cats for a walk. They suggest that you should start the training when your pet is still a kitten and get it used to walking on a harness (not a collar that can be slipped too easily) and lead. You are warned that cats do not take kindly to walking to heel like a dog, and prefer to walk alongside you. Also, long walks, like choke chains, are out of the question.

All this is based on a fundamental misunderstanding about the social life of cats. Adult cats do not go for walks together. They do not explore together, hunt together, flee together or migrate together. When they are on the move they are essentially solitary creatures and find it quite inexplicable that their human owners should wish to indulge in communal walking. If people want to take their pets for walks then they must buy pack animals like dogs, for which group movement is the most natural thing on earth. But cat owners must walk alone.

And yet . . . certain cat owners have reported that *their* cats, unlike others, do like to accompany them on short walks. How can we explain this? If these cases are investigated it is nearly always found that the cats in question are not on leads but are simply following in their owners' footsteps. And these footsteps are nearly always progressing along a well-known garden path or country lane. The village cat owner sets off from home and finds the pet cat tagging along. After a while, the cat gives up and returns to its familiar territory. This is nothing like a synchronized, long-distance, man-and-dog walk and should not be confused with it, but it is a minor walk of sorts and demands some interpretation.

The explanation is found in the behaviour of half-grown kittens. When they have arrived at the fully mobile stage of their development, but have not yet ventured off on their own, they may accompany their mother on short trips away from the 'nest'. She will slow her pace down for them and keep a close eye on them as they amble along near her, but she will not let them get too far away from the home base. When adult cats follow their owners they are reverting to this half-grown kitten stage. For domesticated felines remain 'part-kitten' all through their lives, and even though they may be middle-aged in feline terms they still look upon their human owners as their mothers. So they follow their pseudo-parents as they set off for the village shops, until they feel themselves getting too far from the 'nest', and then break off to return to safety.

Many aspects of adult cat behaviour can be explained in this way, the relics of kittenhood remaining with our pets until they are old and senile.

What are the games cats play?

One of the great pleasures of owning a cat is watching it at play. Or playing with it oneself. For hundreds of years this innocent diversion has fascinated even the most learned of men. As long ago as the second century A.D., the Roman historian Lucius Coelius recorded that, when he was free from his studies and more weighty affairs, he was not ashamed to play and sport himself with his cat. The great naturalist Edward Topsel, in the seventeenth century, waxed lyrical about feline play: 'Therefore how she beggeth, playeth, leapeth, looketh, catcheth, tosseth with her foot, riseth up to strings held over her head, sometimes creeping, sometimes lying on the back, playing with one foot, sometimes on the belly, snatching now with mouth, and anon with the foot . . .' Concerned, however, that these words might make him seem too frivolous, in the simple delight he obviously took in playing with his cat, he checks himself with the criticism that 'verily it may well be called an idle man's pastime'. Warming to this thought he then goes on to castigate cat-lovers 'because they which love any beast in a high measure, have so much less charity unto man.'

Michel de Montaigne, a French writer of the same era, managed to avoid this hypocrisy, stating honestly that, 'When I play with my cat who knows whether she diverts herself with me, or I with her. We entertain one another with mutual follies . . . and if I have my time to begin to refuse, she also has hers.' These remarks reveal the irresistible appeal of the playful cat even in an era when felines were generally considered to be evil and dangerous, and were being widely persecuted. Topsel warns that playing with them may destroy the lungs and corrupt the air: 'There was a certain company of Monks much given to nourish and play with Cats, whereby they were so infected, that within a short space none of them were able to say, read, pray, or sing, in all the Monastery . . . ' But despite these ridiculous fears and superstitions, the cat at play continued to weave its magic and enchant all but the most hypochondriac observers.

Some, however, were concerned about the nature of the play activities, almost all of which were seen to be based on some kind of violence. Even the smallest kittens, they noticed, were acting out attacks either on other members of their own species or on prey animals. In the eighteenth century the French naturalist Buffon remarked: 'Young cats are gay, vivacious, frolicksome, and, if nothing was to be apprehended from their claws, would afford excellent amusement to children. But their toying, though always light and agreeable, is never altogether innocent, and is soon converted into habitual malice.' This is a second form of hypocrisy. Not only does Buffon try to relegate the pleasure of watching kittens at play to the level of a childish amusement, but he also suggests that this play is malicious because it involves acting out the killing of prey – the very skill for which mankind domesticated the cat in the first place.

These moral issues, which troubled those who wished to enjoy the company of animals but felt they had to judge them on a set of human values, have caused less concern in recent years. The gradual acceptance of the Darwinian evolutionary philosophy, that enables us to accept each species in its own right and see its actions from its own point of view, has meant that we are released from the burden of interpreting everything animals do in terms of good and evil. If a cat kills a mouse we may feel sorry for the mouse but we no longer accuse the cat of wickedness. Equally, if the mouse was a pest and we are pleased to see the end of it, we do not praise the cat for the saintly way in which it has fulfilled its duty to its household. Our whole attitude has changed. We now see the cat's actions as part of its natural specialization as a predatory carnivore, and we recognize that in ridding our houses of mice it is neither 'malicious' and 'vicious' on the one hand, nor 'loyal' and 'responsible' on the other. It is merely a cat being a cat.

With this new approach we are able to sit back and enjoy the delightful escapades of young kittens at play without any moral posturing. We are able to become objective observers of the patterns of play and to take pleasure in their endless variations on central themes. Four of these have been identified.

The earliest to develop is that of play-fighting. At about three weeks the kittens start to engage in rough-and-tumble actions with their litter-mates. They jump on one another, roll over on their backs and grapple. No one gets hurt. This is because at first they lack the strength to hurt, and when they do acquire it they quickly learn that a too-powerful play-attack ends the enjoyable encounter. So they perfect the art of inhibited assault. By the age of four weeks the play-fighting becomes more elaborate, with chasing, pouncing, clasping with the front legs and vigorous kicking with the hind legs. And now the other main play-themes are added, each connected with a different kind of prey-hunting. They have been given the names of 'the mouse-pounce', 'the bird-swat' and 'the fish-scoop'.

The mouse-pounce involves hiding, crouching, creeping forward, and then rushing and pouncing on an imaginary rodent, usually its mother's twitching tail or a small object lying on the ground. The bird-swat includes the same approach, but then ends with an upward leap and a sharp blow with the front foot. The stimuli that trigger this action are usually moving objects that hang down from above, or toys that are thrown to the kittens by their owners. The fish-scoop occurs when the object lying on the ground is very static. The kitten suddenly flings out a paw and scoops the object up into the air and backwards over its shoulder. It then turns and pounces on it triumphantly, as if a fish scooped up from a river or stream has been landed on the bank and must be secured before it wriggles its way back to the safety of the water.

During these play bouts the kitten's imagination is put to full use. Anything small that moves easily may be accepted as a victim. Expensive toys are available in the form of wind-up mice, tinkling cylinders and catnip-soaked balls, and both young kittens and older cats may react to these with great intensity. This interest, however, may be rather brief, for these toys usually lack two essential qualities. They are too hard and too heavy. The ideal toy is very light, so that only a small amount of effort moves it a long way, and very soft, so that sharp feline claws and teeth can sink into it in a satisfying way. Ironically, this means that the most exciting objects for play are also the simplest and the cheapest. A piece of silver wrapping-paper rolled up into a tight ball, or the traditional ball of wool, provides the greatest reward. One owner after another makes the amused discovery that these simple objects will keep the playful cat or kitten occupied much longer than any fancy toy.

All cats show the four basic patterns of play described here, but in addition each pet feline may develop its own special games. These become almost like rituals as the cat grows older – little routines that reward the animal because they involve it in a social interaction with its owners or their guests. Thomas Huxley, the great biologist, whose household was dominated by a long series of cats over a period of forty years, described how one of them, a young tabby tom-cat, developed the alarming game of jumping on the shoulders of his dinner-guests and refusing to dismount until they fed him some titbit. It was not that the animal was hungry. It was the shock impact of the game that provided the reward.

One owner discovered another routine. If he put down sheets of newspaper in the kitchen to keep the floor clean on wet days, one of his cats would back up to the far wall and then launch herself as fast as she could at the papers. The moment she hit one of the papers, she braked and went into a long skid, sliding right across the kitchen floor to the other wall, which she thumped into, still standing on her 'magic carpet'. After this she would return to the far wall and wait for the papers to be put back into place, so she could repeat the game.

Another owner discovered that if he put a line of coins on his sideboard his cat would knock them down one by one. Eventually he managed to turn this into a special trick, with the cat knocking down a coin each time his owner clicked his fingers. The same cat enjoyed jumping from chair to chair when his owner pointed at each in turn.

The more one talks to individual cat owners, the greater the variety of cat personalities one finds. It is true that all cats share many features of their behaviour, down to the tiniest detail. But when it comes to playtime, each cat seems to have its own personal, idiosyncratic way of embellishing its playful interactions with its owners. If it is lucky, it will have owners who are of an equally playful frame of mind.

Why do white cats make bad mothers?

This is because they often do not hear their kittens calling to them and they ignore their cries for attention. However, this is not due to white cats being stupid or careless mothers, but to the fact that a large proportion of them are deaf and are therefore unaware of the problems of their mewing offspring.

Not all white cats are deaf, however, and owners of these animals should carry out some simple noise tests to find out whether they are lucky or not. It is the blue-eyed white cats that are most prone to deafness. Those with orange eyes are much more likely to be able to hear.

It is important when testing a cat's hearing to ensure that you make the noise to check its reactions out of sight of the cat. And it is also important not to make the noise by stamping or banging against a hard surface, because this can set up vibrations that even a totally deaf cat can detect through the sensitive pads of its feet. But if the cat can see nothing and feel nothing and yet it still reacts to the loud noise you make, then yours is one of the fortunate, hearing white cats.

If, on the other hand, your cat is one of the deaf ones, then there is nothing you can do to help it. Its cochlea, that vital, snail-shaped organ in the inner ear, will have started to degenerate a few days after birth, and the deterioration is completely irreversible. It is a genetically-linked defect and will be passed on to the white offspring of the deaf mother. It is therefore important not to breed from such cats if possible. In this way, the small proportion of white cats that *can* hear will become more common and the defect could, in theory, be wiped out after a few generations.

The particular combination of white fur and blue eyes seems to be the crucial one, and this is brought home vividly in the case of odd-eyed cats. Sometimes a white cat is born with one blue eye and one orange eye. In such cases, tests show that only the ear on the side of the blue eye is deaf. The ear on the side of the orange eye works perfectly well in most cases. Such cats

63

may be at a disadvantage when hunting, because their sense of directional sound will be poor, but in other respects they can lead normal lives and make good mothers.

Owners of deaf white cats report that their pets are brilliant at compensating for their genetic disability. They become extra sensitive to tiny vibrations made by sounds and can almost 'hear through their feet'. Their watchfulness is also dramatically increased, so that they can make maximum use of their excellent sense of vision. Indeed it is not such a great tragedy to discover that a pet cat is deaf, although there is a sad weakening of the intimate communication system that cat owners and their cats enjoy sharing. But, like the cat itself, the owners can learn to become more visual in their feline exchanges, using gestures and movements where otherwise they might have used the human voice.

Are tortoiseshell cats always female?

Nearly always. The chances of finding a male tortoiseshell have been calculated at about 200 to 1. They may be extremely rare but they do exist. This poses two questions: why are almost all tortoiseshells females, and why, if males are so unfavoured in this colour-form, do they appear at all?

First, what exactly is a tortoiseshell cat? Although there are some variations, it is essentially a cat that displays an irregular pattern of black and red fur. 'Red' is the technical term for what most people would call ginger, orange or marmalade. Red cats are essentially red tabbies, with the red coloration in dark and light bands rather than uniformly spread. So a tortoiseshell cat is in reality a cat that is part black and part red tabby, giving it a tri-coloured look.

What makes the sex distribution of these cats so odd is that normally only a female kitten can display black patches inherited from one parent and red tabby patches inherited from the other. This is because the genes controlling these particular colour-forms are both carried on the X chromosomes, the red gene on one and the non-red gene on the other. The catch is that only females have two X chromosomes, so only females can display the red plus non-red tortoiseshell combination. Males have instead one X chromosome and one small Y chromosome, which means that on their single X they carry either the red *or* the non-red gene, but cannot have both. So they are either all-over red tabby or all-over black.

If this is the case, then how can any male tortoiseshells exist at all? The answer is that occasionally there is a minor genetic error and a male cat develops with the combination XXY. The double X gives it the chance to be red and black, while the Y gives it male characteristics. It does, however, have a problem because its masculinity leaves a lot to be desired. To start with, it is sterile. Also its behaviour is extremely odd. It acts like a masculinized female rather than a true male.

One particular male tortoiseshell that was observed in a

colony of cats revealed a strange personality. It was nonchalant in its dealings with other cats, disdainfully ignoring the usual status battles, which were nearly always between males or between females – there was little social fighting across the genders. Perhaps because the tortoiseshell male was neither fully male nor fully female, it did not feel the need to compete in these single-sex pecking-order disputes.

In other respects it was also peculiar. It did not start to spray urine at the age when any typical male would have done so. It did not court or attempt to mate with females on heat, even though it appeared to be anatomically well equipped to do so. It did, however, allow young tom-cats to mount and attempt to mate with it.

When it had grown older it did show a little interest in females and even deigned to mate with a few, though never with much enthusiasm. It also sprayed urine in a desultory fashion, but never behaved like a full-blooded tom at any stage. Once it was experimentally isolated with a highly-sexed female and was observed to mate several times, but the female failed to become pregnant, confirming the typical male tortoiseshell infertility.

So, although it is not true to say that *all* tortoiseshell cats are females, it is true to say that they are all feminine – even the rare males. And it is probably true to add that no tortoiseshell cat has ever fathered a litter of kittens.

There is one compensation, however, for the unfortunate tortoiseshell toms. Their great rarity has given them a special value in times past, so that they have often escaped the indifference and persecution that has befallen the common-place moggies. In Celtic countries it was always considered a good omen if one of these cats decided to settle in the home. In England there was a belief that warts could be removed simply by rubbing them with the tail of a tortoiseshell tom during the month of May. And Japanese fishermen would pay huge sums for a tortoiseshell tom, to keep as a ship's cat, for it was thought it would protect the crew from the ghosts of their ancestors and the vessel itself from storms.

So, although these cats may be doomed to a disappointing sex life, in other respects they have fared remarkably well.

Can a litter of kittens have more than one father?

Yes, this is possible and it even has a name: *superfecundation*. A glance at the mating behaviour of cats tells why. When the female comes into heat, her calling and her sexual fragrance attract tom-cats from all around. They gather near her and squabble among themselves with much caterwauling. Then one of them approaches her and mates. The act of copulation usually only takes about five seconds, ejaculation occurring as soon as the male has entered the female. After a rest of about twenty minutes, they copulate again and this process is repeated approximately seven times, by which stage the male is usually satiated.

Some females develop a special attachment to one particular tom-cat and reject other suitors, waiting for the favoured male to become sexually aroused again. But it is just as likely that she will allow one male after another to mount her until her whole circle of admirers has been accommodated. This means that her reproductive tract will contain a mixture of sperm from several sources and it becomes almost a matter of chance as to which particular male's sperm fertilizes each of her shed eggs.

The result of this is sometimes a multi-patterned litter of kittens, which some owners mistakenly consider to be the outcome of 'genetic variety' within the make-up of their female and an unknown 'husband'. But the wildly differing kittens may instead be the product of the sexual promiscuity of their female.

This is essentially a phenomenon of domestic cats, because the territories of wild cats are so much bigger, and the chances of a whole group of tom-cats coming together in one spot when a wild female is on heat are more remote. Superfecundation is most likely to occur in town and city cats, where the individual territories have become so reduced in size that the odour of a sexually active female can easily be detected by a whole collection of different males. Were it not for the extreme aggression that subsequently erupts when the males come too close to one another, superfecundation would undoubtedly be even more common than it is, but some males will never dare to risk a mating with a dominant tom-cat watching from nearby. On the other hand, if female cats were not so sexually voracious, superfecundation would also be far less common. If the queen cat was satisfied from her seven matings with one tom, she would leave the other males in the lurch and make for home. But typically she refuses to do this, writhing on the ground and inviting more and more matings until her period of heat has passed. By this time, with the top tom-cats so sexually exhausted, even some of the masculine runts may risk a quick mating.

There is a feline phenomenon even stranger than superfecundation and that is *superfetation*. Female cats are such powerful breeding machines that some of them may even come into heat while they are pregnant. It is one of the basic rules of reproductive behaviour that the condition of pregnancy suppresses a female's sexual physiology, but female cats break this golden rule. In about one out of ten, when there is a low level of pregnancy hormone in the system, there is another phase of sexual receptivity actually *during* the pregnancy cycle. Feline pregnancy lasts nine weeks, and the additional heats usually occur after three or six weeks. These send the expectant mothers out on the tiles again where, if they are mated once more, they will be fertilized again and then carry two litters at two different stages of development.

In these cases, both sets of kittens continue to develop alongside one another, with the later group three or six weeks behind the early one. This creates two alternative problems for the mother-to-be. When she starts to give birth to the older litter, the upheaval of delivery may lead to the younger litter being ejected as well. If this happens they are so premature that they nearly always die. If, on the other hand, they manage to hang on inside the uterus, they may be born successfully at full term three or six weeks later. This causes a second type of problem – an almost impossible demand for nipples and milk supply. But if the female is able to cope with all or part of this added maternal burden she can, of course, contribute even more spectacularly to the feline population explosion.

Will one female cat feed another one's kittens?

Yes, she will. If a nursing mother has a normal-sized litter it is possible to add one or two orphaned kittens to it without much difficulty. They would probably be accepted simply by placing them, mewing plaintively, near her nest-box. Her maternal instincts would be so strong that she would be unable to resist their calls for help and would soon approach them, pick them up individually in her mouth and place them in her bed. There she would lick them and give them her scent and then allow them to feed alongside her own kittens.

Some breeders fear that this method might not always be successful, so they give the process a little assistance. They do this by waiting for the mother to leave the nest. While she is away feeding they take the strange kittens and rub them gently in the bedding that carries the female's scent. Then they leave them there, in among her own kittens, and when she returns the chances are that she will calmly lie down and let all the kittens feed from her without examining them in detail. Mother cats do not seem to be very efficient at counting their kittens and if the newcomers have become covered in the 'home scent', all is well.

Where a large number of female cats are kept together in a cattery, observers have noticed that the kittens born there are often shared out between the mothers. These group-living females show remarkable degrees of social tolerance and sometimes take up residence in large, communal nests, carrying all their kittens in there and piling them up in a huge, squirming mass. On one occasion no fewer than six females with eighteen kittens established a communal nest of this type and each female allowed the other mothers to offer their milk to any kittens whenever they felt like it. Normally, when there is a single mother cat, each kitten is the 'owner' of its own personal nipple and always returns to the same nipple every time it feeds. But in these nursery nests, the kittens took the first nipple they came across, regardless of whether it was in a familiar position on the female's belly, or even which belly it was. This free-and-easy arrangement produced strong, healthy kittens that flourished because of the division of labour of the mother cats. There was only one drawback and that concerned the weaker kittens that sometimes found themselves at the bottom of a pile of bodies and unable to breathe. An occasional casualty from suffocation was recorded, but in other respects the group maternity-home worked extremely efficiently.

In the wild such behaviour would normally never occur because of the large size of each adult cat's territory. For one litter of kittens to encounter another, or for one nursing mother to come close to another's nest, would be a rare occurrence. As a result there would have been little or no evolutionary pressure on cats to develop an anti-stranger reaction where kittens are concerned. Hence the easy sharing of kittens in a cattery where the adult females have already, through overcrowding, come to tolerate one another's presence.

Although this altruistic caring for other cats' kittens is abnormal for many felines, it does show how, under freak conditions of extreme crowding, it might be possible for a group of wild cats to start behaving like a pride of lions. Indeed, it has been suggested that this is precisely how lion prides arose, many years ago on the prey-rich plains of Africa, where the surplus of food led to an unusual increase in the lion population.

Why do tom-cats kill kittens?

As a father, the tom-cat has a bad reputation. For centuries he has been looked upon as a sex maniac whose only interest in kittens is to kill them if he gets half a chance. This image of the male owes its origin to the writings of the great historian Herodotus, following his visit to ancient Egypt two and a half thousand years ago. Amazed by the Egyptians' devotion to their cat population, he felt inspired to comment on certain aspects of the behaviour of the felines.

Among his observations is the following assessment of the sexual cunning of the tom-cat: 'As the females when they have kittened no longer seek the company of the males, these last, to obtain once more their companionship, practise a curious artifice. They seize the kittens, carry them off, and kill them; but do not eat them afterwards. Upon this the females, being deprived of their young and longing to supply their place, seek the males once more, since they are particularly fond of their offspring.'

In other words, the sex-mad tom-cats destroy the litters of kittens in order to get the females back on heat again more quickly. This story has lasted well during the past two millennia and many people still believe it, so that tom-cats are always kept carefully away from nursing mother cats and their young kittens, in case the urge to commit lust-inspired infanticide overcomes them. Nobody has commented on any possible biological advantage of such a reaction on the part of tom-cats, or why the males should want to eliminate their own genetic progeny. So what is the truth?

Observations of European wild cats, which belong to the same species as the domestic cat, reveal that, far from being kitten-killers, the males sometimes actively participate in rearing the young. One tom was seen to carry his own food to the entrance of the den in which his female had given birth and place it there for her. Another tom did the same thing, supplying his female with food while she was unable to leave the nest

71

during the first days after producing her litter. He also became very defensive and threatened human visitors in a way that he had not done before the young were born. Both these cat families were in zoos, where the proximity of the male was forced on the female and where, if anywhere, one might have expected to see tom-cat aggression towards the young.

In the wild, where cats have huge territories, the chances of a tom-cat coming across a female in her den with her kittens is remote, so there is little opportunity for either paternal care or paternal infanticide. In the crowded conditions of the zoo or the human city, greater proximity increases the likelihood of tom-cat/kitten encounters and when these happen one of four reactions occurs:

1 The male simply ignores the kittens.
2 The male behaves paternally towards them, as in the case of the zoo cats.
3 The female attacks the male as soon as he approaches her nest, and drives him away before he can reveal how he would have responded to the kittens.
4 The male kills the kittens.

Although this fourth reaction is the traditionally accepted one, it is in reality extremely rare. Nearly all the encounters end in one of the other three ways. But clearly the old tale from Herodotus would not have survived 2,500 years without any supporting evidence whatsoever, so how can the rare cases that have kept the story going be explained?

The answer seems to be that a female cat sometimes experiences a 'false heat' a few weeks after she has given birth. If a tom-cat is nearby this excites him tremendously, but the female usually fights with him and drives him off. Now in a great state of sexual arousal, the frustrated tom is desperate. If he meets a small kitten at this stage he may try to mount it and mate with it. The low, crouched posture of the kitten is similar to that of the sexually responsive adult female cat. This, and the kitten's inability to move away quickly when the male mounts it, act as sexual signals to the over-excited tom-cat and seal the fate of the unfortunate kitten. The male does not attack it but, when mounting the tiny animal, simply performs

72

the perfectly normal neck-bite that he employs when copulating with a female. To the kitten this feels just like its mother's maternal grabbing, so it does not struggle. Indeed, it responds by remaining very still. This is the specific sexual signal from the adult female that tells the male that she is ready to mate. The misunderstanding causes disaster when the mounted tom-cat discovers that the kitten is too small for mating. He cannot manoeuvre himself into the correct position. His response to this problem is to grip the kitten's neck tighter and tighter, as if he is dealing with an awkward adult mate. In the process he accidentally crunches the kitten's tiny, delicate head and it dies.

Once it has been killed, the kitten may trigger off a new reaction. Dead kittens are often devoured by their parents seemingly as a way of keeping the nest clean. So the victim of the tom-cat's sexual frustration may now be eaten, as the final act of this gruesome misfiring of the feline reproductive sequence. It is these rare occurrences that have led to stories of tom-cat cannibalism – and to stories that paint the male feline as a savage monster bent on slaughtering and consuming his own children. For so many animal fallacies, it is the rare event that becomes established as the 'norm' in popular animal lore, and usually – as in this case – with the animal motives involved luridly exaggerated or distorted.

How long do cats continue to breed?

The short answer is: for a very long time. Tom-cats have been known to produce offspring at the advanced feline age of sixteen years. This is equivalent to a human male becoming a father in his late seventies.

Female cats have been known to give birth when twelve years old. For a human female this would be like having a baby in her mid-sixties. The oldest known woman to give birth was fifty-seven years old, which is the equivalent of only nine feline years. The more typical female, experiencing the menopause at fifty-one, would be the equivalent of a female cat of only seven years. This means that cats remain fertile longer than we do, in relative terms.

Not to exaggerate the cat's breeding abilities, it must be recorded that from the age of eight until twelve years there is a gradual decline in the number of kittens produced in each litter, so the reproductive apparatus is beginning to show signs of slowing down at this stage, and only the strongest and healthiest of moggies can stay the full course. Pedigree cats, because they lack 'hybrid vigour', are not so long-lasting.

For those who like to make comparisons between their pets' ages and their own, bearing in mind that the figures are only a rough guide, the following table may be of interest. The ages are given in years:

Your cat's age	Your own age
1	15
2	25
4	40
7	50
10	60
15	75
20	105
30	120

Are there contraceptives for cats?

Yes, there are. Because cats, like people, are breeding too fast there has been a concerted effort to provide them with a contraceptive pill similar to the one we use. A few years ago this was extremely popular, but since the initial boom in feline birth pills there has been a decline in interest in favour of the more drastic method of neutering. This is partly because, in early field trials with stray cats, it was discovered that the animals were developing side-effects of an unpleasant kind, and partly because there is a less than 100 per cent efficiency. Since stray cat populations can only be dosed with the birth pill via their food, there is always the chance that certain cats will avoid the treated meals provided for them and scavenge or catch prey for themselves. Such individuals will then continue to breed, and the numbers will not sink as rapidly as the population controllers would like.

There are several kinds of contraceptive pills available, and they act in slightly different ways. The *progestogens* have the same effect on the cat's body as the natural pregnancy hormone, progesterone. They give the female cat a false pregnancy, complete with all the usual accompanying symptoms, such as increased appetite and increased weight. They can be administered either as simple tablets or as a special, long-acting injection. But in both instances there are dangers of infection and for this reason other methods have since been tried.

A modified version of this treatment employing weaker progestogens has been tested recently and there is now a much safer pill of this type available. Called *proligesterone*, its side-effects appear to be much less damaging.

A different approach is to inhibit the hormone which starts off the female sexual cycle. This hormone, called gonadotrophin, can be suppressed by certain drugs that stop the oestrus cycle without causing serious side-effects. This is a new method and is being developed further with some optimism.

75

A non-chemical method is also possible, but requires skilful, expert handling. This involves stimulating a female cat that is on heat with a glass rod, so that her body is fooled into reacting as if she has been mated by a tom-cat. Because it is the mating act in cats that induces ovulation, it is possible in this way to start the female cat's ovulation as if she is carrying male sperm. Because she is not, the eggs she sheds will be wasted and contraception will have been achieved. Her sexual appetite will pass and she will be quiet again until her next heat. As before, however, she will have to go through a phantom pregnancy as a result of this treatment.

All these methods require veterinary assistance and should not be attempted without professional help or approved prescriptions. There is no doubt, though, that within the next half-century we will see this type of biological control of feline populations perfected.

How does being neutered affect a cat's behaviour?

It has become increasingly common to remove the sex organs of both male and female domestic cats. In books written by vets on the subject of cat 'care' and cat 'health', it is now standard practice to refer to the spaying of females and the castration of males as minor, routine operations. 'Unless you are setting up a breeding stud, all pet toms should be castrated,' is a typical comment. What is not recorded is the tom-cats' attitude to this helpful form of health care. It is just possible that, given the choice, they might prefer the risk of an occasional torn ear or scratched nose to the certainty of a totally sexless adult life.

How has it come about that we are prepared to describe a serious physical mutilation as a trivial adjustment? Why are we so ready to treat as a minor operation an alteration which involves a major transformation in the cat's lifestyle and personality? The answer is that, for many of us, the cat has become a living toy rather than a real animal. We enjoy its company but we are not prepared to tolerate any inconvenience. So, if it is a male, we cut off its testicles; if it is a female we cut out its uterus and its ovaries; and if we are house-proud, we also cut out the claws of both sexes. Our sexless, clawless cats will now give us the perfect companionship we seek. They will not yowl, wander, mate or engage in sexual brawling; they will not spray their sexual scents; they will not tear precious fabrics; nor will they be able to hunt, kill or climb with any efficiency. In short, they will not be true cats, but they will undeniably make more convenient pets. In the end it all comes down to a matter of priorities. How much trouble are we prepared to go to for the privilege of sharing our lives with feline companions?

In order to persuade us to carry our cats off to the nearest surgery for 'altering', the many benefits of the operation are extolled at length. Apart from eliminating the tiresome sexual preoccupations of our pets, it will also make them more affectionate and more playful. Their average lifespan will be increased by two or three years. They will become generally more docile and less demanding. The surgeon's knife beckons invitingly.

Should we hesitate, there is one final threat to drive us on: the spectre of over-population. If we fail to remove our cats' sex organs, they will fill the world with thousands of unwanted kittens. If this were true it would be a powerful argument, but it is not. There is an alternative. It is easy to prevent cats breeding without de-sexing them. The most obvious way is to keep them indoors at times of sexual activity. This does, however, prove so difficult in most cases that it is not recommended. The better way to handle the situation is to render the cats infertile without actually neutering them. For the female this means cutting or tying her fallopian tubes. This prevents her from becoming pregnant but does not interfere with her love-life. For the male it means a vasectomy – the cutting or tying of the male's sperm ducts. This prevents him from supplying sperm to fertilize his females, but again it does nothing else. It does not make him docile or lazy, nor does it interfere with his sexual activities.

The existence of this contraceptive technique immediately puts cat owners on the spot. It prevents those who do neuter their pets from claiming that they are simply responsible citizens who wish to assist in the elimination of starving strays. The thousands of strays created by reckless, thoughtlessly uncontrolled cat-breeding could all have been prevented by the tube-tying techniques, without resorting to the full butchery of neutering. The owners are forced to admit honestly that they are having their cats' sex organs cut out for purely selfish reasons – to make them less restless, noisy and, in the case of toms, less smelly and belligerent in the mating seasons. If they face this honestly it is somehow less offensive than if they pretend that they are having their pets mutilated for 'the cat's own good'.

Are there any gay cats?

Yes and no. Yes, cats do perform homosexual acts under certain circumstances, but no, they never prefer to mate with members of their own sex if members of the opposite sex are present. Homosexual acts are always second best for them and they are in no sense sexually disabled, as are certain human males or females who are incapable of being aroused sexually by the opposite sex.

If two male or two female cats find themselves together, sexually aroused but lacking suitable mates, one member of the pair may suddenly switch to the mating pattern of the 'wrong' sex. A female may mount another female, showing the masculine neck-bite and sometimes even making the typical male body-thrusts. Similarly, a male may crouch like a female and perform pseudo-female behaviour, being mounted by another tom.

This is simply an overspilling of sexual activity under conditions of extreme frustration, and the animals which have been seen to perform in this way have also been observed to copulate normally afterwards, if mates are provided. If the sexual thwarting becomes acute enough, some cats will even masturbate or attempt to mate with inanimate objects. One cat was observed to attempt copulation with a toy teddy bear, another with a toy rabbit.

In laboratory studies where male cats were kept isolated, awaiting mating tests with females, it was discovered that if one male was placed in a cage belonging to another tom it was often 'raped' by the cage owner. This was not a matter of individual strength but of territorial ownership. Even if the cage owner was a small, weaker cat and the introduced male was large and powerful, it was still the owner which mounted and the visitor which crouched in the female fashion. If the situation was reversed, then the mating roles were also reversed. It was always the territory owner who (literally) came out on top.

Is it possible to catch AIDS from cats?

No, it is not. But it has become difficult to convince those hypochondriacs who also happen to be cat owners that there is no danger. This is because certain newspapers thoughtlessly mentioned that some pet cats in California had been discovered to be suffering from the AIDS virus. These reports were made without checking the facts and without any consideration for the panic they could cause. Inevitably they led to the totally unnecessary deaths of many pet cats, as jittery owners took emergency steps to protect themselves from the dreaded twentieth-century plague.

Their fears were quite unfounded, because the so-called 'Feline AIDS' is caused by a different virus from the one that has attacked humans. True, it belongs to the same group of viruses, but within that group it is only distantly related. So, even if bitten or scratched by a cat that had somehow smeared its teeth or claws with infected blood from its sores, the human victim would still not be able to pick up the disease. There is no evidence from any source that 'Feline AIDS' can infect the human body.

Despite this, scaremongering journalists have managed to cause fear and anxiety among those cat-lovers who are of a 'nervous disposition'. Within hours of the reports appearing in the press, vets and cat sanctuaries were flooded with requests to have cats destroyed or to find them new homes. By the time that the truth had been publicized it was sadly too late for many unfortunate cats, and even now the ghost of the 'Feline AIDS' still stalks the world of cats and cat owners. For the felines themselves it is almost like a modern rebirth of the senseless persecution of the Medieval period, when they were accused of being servants of Satan. We can only hope that common sense will prevail more quickly than it did in the previous instance.

What is the cause of cat phobia?

For those of us who live with a friendly cat it is hard to understand people who suffer from a terror of encountering felines at
close quarters. This fear of cats, or *ailurophobia* to give it its
technical name, is rare, but when it does occur it can cause
untold misery for the sufferer and it is worth examining how it
begins and how it can be cured.

One way it can start is through a childhood trauma – a
sudden unpleasant shock involving a cat or a kitten. When we
are very young we see a fluffy kitten as something especially
soft and cuddly and we have a strong desire to pick it up and
hold it tight. Kittens sometimes take badly to this over-zealous
embrace and strike out with their sharp claws. The idea that
something so apparently soft and harmless has pain-inflicting
daggers on the ends of the feet is enough to disturb certain
infants and to make them distrust the approaches of all felines.
There is a kind of infantile betrayal – the kitten says, 'I am all
soft,' and then, when this statement has been fully trusted by
the child, the animal strikes out painfully and draws blood.
This is so unexpected when it is encountered for the first time
that it feels like a deliberate deception. Distrust can then rise
to the level of terror if cats are subsequently greatly avoided, so
that they never become familiar to the growing child. Soon a
full-blown phobia has developed.

A second way in which cat phobia can arise stems from an
irrational fear on the part of parents that the family cat may try
to smother the newly-arrived baby, by sitting on top of its face
while the child lies sleeping in its cot. This old wives' tale is
amazingly persistent, despite the fact that no cat could possibly
relax and sleep on top of a squirming, suffocating baby. As a
result, many an infant may experience a shrieking mother
rushing into the nursery and yelling at the cat to leave the
room. These early associations between cats and panic may
leave their mark and resurface later in the life of the child.

These explanations cannot be the whole answer, however,

because it still remains to be explained why it is that human females are much more prone to ailurophobia than human males. There must be some hidden sexual factor involved, as though the soft-furred (and therefore sexy) cat has come to stand for sexual violence and rape, via its savagely sharp claws and canine teeth. This more psychoanalytical explanation may seem far-fetched, but it is important to realize that feline terms have often been given some sort of sexual connotation (sex kittens, pussy as slang for female genitals, and cathouse for brothel). If the cat is sexy, then fear of cats could have something to do with an abnormally suppressed sex drive.

How does the cat-hater show the feelings of fear? And what is it about the cat that is the specific trigger for the irrational panics? One important factor seems to be the tendency of the cat to 'jump up unexpectedly' and to behave in an unpredictable way when at close quarters. This feature of feline behaviour is mentioned time and again in investigations of cat phobics. Sadly for them, their response to it works against them and encourages the very behaviour they fear most. Because they are so terrified, they sit very, very still. But cats much prefer placid, stationary bodies on which to fall asleep. So the more frozen in horror a human being is, the more likely the cat is to leap up and try to settle down on the static lap. When this happens to a true phobic the results can be dramatic with screams and sometimes outbursts of weeping.

It has been suggested that the special fear of the cat jumping up on them in an unexpected way is the result of cat phobics' general dislike of spontaneity and fear of the suddenly surprising. But it seems more likely that this fear has more to do with the childhood horror of seeing the parent scream at the 'smothering' cat that has just jumped up on to a cot or bed.

The cure for cat phobia is straightforward enough, but distressing for the patient. It requires a series of step-by-step familiarization 'lessons', in which at first things only remotely feline are presented to the victim. These may be simply photographs of kittens or cats, or toy animals. After a while a kitten is placed in a small, secure cage and left on the far side of a room, while the phobic is gently reassured that it cannot get near. Gradually, the animal is moved nearer and day by day the phobia can be reduced in intensity until eventually the victim can actually hold a kitten. After this, the longer spent in the company of cats the better, but always with the careful avoidance of any sudden, unanticipated move. After a few months of therapy it is usual for even the most intense form of cat phobia to disappear. Sadly, many sufferers believe that there is no cure and can never be one. For them there is a needless, lifelong fear of encountering a strange cat, a fear that sometimes ends with them refusing to go out of doors at all. Their condition is beyond reason, but it is certainly not, as they believe, beyond cure.

Are there ideal cats for allergy sufferers?

Up until the 1950s, it was difficult for any human beings who suffered from an allergic response to cats to become cat owners, no matter how much they longed to share their lives with a feline companion. But since then things have changed, and if they are prepared to go to a little trouble and expense they can now acquire a cat that will almost certainly give them no problems.

There are now two breeds of cat available that do not appear to cause allergic responses, which with an ordinary cat would lead to breathing difficulties and an asthmatic condition. The two breeds in question are the Cornish Rex and the Sphynx.

The Cornish Rex was discovered in 1950 when it was noticed that a cat with the unusual name of Kallibunker did not have normal feline fur. Kallibunker's coat was short, sparse and curly, and it was quickly realized that he might be the forerunner of an entirely new breed of pedigree cat. This is indeed what happened and, from his humble Cornish origins, Kallibunker became the founding father of the Rex dynasty.

The remarkable feature of Kallibunker's fur was that it completely lacked the usual long guard hairs found on all other cats. These are the hairs that appear to cause the allergic response in human sufferers, so it looked as if the Rex would become the ideal breed for such people to own. Several who tried keeping the cats reported delightedly that this was the case. Whether *all* asthmatics and allergy sufferers would find the Rex cat suitable has yet to be proved, since the breed has remained comparatively rare. This is because, despite its great charm, it does look rather odd to most cat-lovers.

Those who have been able to overlook its skimpy fur, which gives it a gangling, half-naked appearance, insist that in personality it is a sheer delight, retaining an almost kittenish playfulness even when adult. Some owners have claimed that their Cornish Rex cats wag their tails when pleased, like dogs, although this is hard to believe. Nevertheless, this supposed trait and their tight, curly hair have given rise to the use of the name 'Poodle cats' as a popular term for them.

Amazingly, cats with similar genes were found in Germany and when these were crossed with the Cornish Rex specimens they produced typical curly offspring. So the German Rex would also be a suitable cat for an allergy sufferer. This does not apply, however, to the Devon Rex cat, another curly-coated breed, discovered in 1960, not far from the original Cornish Rex home. Despite its close proximity, it was discovered that this breed owed its curly coat to a different gene and close inspection revealed that, unlike the Cornish and German breeds, this one did have a few long guard hairs. It would probably still be better for an asthmatic than other, fully-furred breeds, but there is little point in taking a risk with it when there is the more suitable Cornish Rex available.

If even the Cornish Rex causes doubts and worries, then there is only one option left: the bizarre but very friendly Sphynx Cat. This is an almost naked cat, and even the most sensitive allergy sufferers would be unable to generate much of a reaction to this remarkable animal. It originates from Canada, where a hairless kitten was born in 1966 and caused a sensation. In the resulting breed, the body is covered with a short, soft down in place of the usual fur and as the cat grows up this down persists only on the extremities. As a result, its face appears to be covered in suede or velvet and it feels like soft moss to the touch. The naked skin of its trunk reveals every wrinkle and crease as it moves about and to many eyes this makes it the ugliest cat in existence. But it is still a cat and a particularly affectionate one, making a most rewarding pet if you can overlook its strange nudity. One solution to this, of course, is to make it a coat of some non-allergic material. This would have the double value of hiding its stark skin and of giving it back some of its missing insulation. Definitely not a cat for someone whose house lacks central heating, but certainly an excellent breed for the allergic and the asthmatic would-be cat owner.

How many kinds of hairs do cats have?

A wild cat has four kinds: down hairs, awn hairs, guard hairs and vibrissae. There may be as many as two hundred hairs per square millimetre, giving the cat an excellent fur coat that can protect it from even the most severe night air.

The *down hairs* are the ones closest to the skin and it is their primary task to keep the animal warm and to conserve its precious body heat. These are the shortest, thinnest and softest of the hairs. They have roughly the same diameter down their whole length, but instead of being straight they have many short undulations, making them appear crimped or crinkled when viewed under a magnifying lens. It is the soft and curly quality of this undercoat, or underfur, that gives it its excellent heat-retaining property.

The *awn hairs* form the middle-coat. They are intermediate between the soft underfur and the guard hairs of the topcoat. Their task is partly insulatory and partly protective. They are bristly with a slight swelling towards the tip, before the final tapering-off. Some authorities subdivide them into three types – the down-awn hairs, the awn hairs and the guard-awn hairs – but these subtle distinctions are of little value.

The *guard hairs* form the protective topcoat. They are the longest and thickest of the ordinary body hairs and serve to protect the underfur from the outside elements, keeping it dry and snug. These hairs are straight and evenly tapered along their length.

The *vibrissae* are the greatly enlarged and toughened hairs employed as sensitive organs of touch. These specialized tactile hairs form the whiskers of the upper lips, and are also found on the cheeks and the chin, over the eyes and on the wrists of the forelegs. Compared with the other types of hair there are very few of them, but they play a vital role when the cat is exploring in poor light, or is hunting.

Of the three types of general body fur on the wild cat, the down hairs are the most numerous. For every thousand down hairs there will only be about three hundred awn hairs and twenty guard hairs. But these ratios vary enormously with the different breeds of pedigree cats. This is because these felines have been carefully selected for their special kinds of coats. Some are fine and thin, others short and coarse, or long and fluffy. The differences are due to exaggerations and reductions of the different types of hair.

Pedigree long-haired cats, for example, have excessively lengthy guard hairs, measuring up to 5 inches, and greatly elongated down hairs, but no awn hairs. Some short-haired breeds have guard hairs that are less than 2 inches in length, sparse awn hairs and no down hairs. Wirehair cats have all three types of body hair, but they are all short and curly. The strange Cornish Rex cats have no guard hairs and only very short, curly awn and down hairs. The Devon Rex has all three types of body hair, but they are all reduced to the quality of down hairs. The amazing naked cat – the Canadian Sphynx – lacks both guard and awn hairs and has only a soft fuzz of down hairs on its extremities.

So selective breeding has played havoc with the natural coat of the cat, producing types of animal that would not all thrive in the wild today. Some would suffer from the cold, others from the heat, and still others would become badly matted and tangled without their daily grooming. Fortunately for these pedigree breeds there are usually plenty of human slaves around to tend to their needs and comforts and, should the worst happen and the animals be forced to fend for themselves as strays, changes would soon take place. They themselves might suffer from the climate, but if they managed to survive and interbreed the chances are that in a few generations their offspring would have reverted to wild-type coats once again, as a result of the inevitable mixing that would occur among the stray cat colonies.

Why do so many black cats have a few white hairs?

Anyone owning an ordinary black moggie, as distinct from a pedigree 'Black Shorthair', may well have noticed that it boasts a small patch of white hairs, sometimes boldly visible and sometimes barely perceptible. Occasionally an otherwise totally black cat may have a single white whisker. More commonly, there is a touch of white on the chest. Why should this be?

It is certainly no accident. In fact it is a remnant of a disastrous period in the history of European felines. The origins of the black cat, as a distinct colour type, have been traced back to the ancient Phoenicians, who sneaked some of the sacred cats out of Egypt and began trading in them around the Mediterranean. During their travels they appear to have developed a black variety which became extremely popular, perhaps because its natural nocturnal camouflage assisted it to become a more efficient mouser and ratter. The black cat spread all over Europe until, in medieval times, it became associated with black magic and sorcery. For several centuries after this it was persecuted. The Christian Church organized annual burning-cats-alive ceremonies on the day of the Feast of St John. For these cruel rituals the most wicked and depraved of 'Satan's felines' were strongly preferred and all-black cats were eagerly sought out for the flames. But these cats had to be totally black to be really evil, in the minds of the pious worshippers. Any touch of white on their black coats might be taken as a sign that they were not, after all, cats consecrated to the Devil.

As a result of this distinction, cats that were totally black became less and less common, while those that were black with a touch of white survived. Religion acted as a powerful selection pressure on feline coloration.

By the seventeenth century, when this persecution of cats was beginning to wane, a new danger arose. It was now believed that they – or vital parts of them – were infallible cures for a whole variety of ailments and weaknesses. The tail of an all-black cat, severed and buried under the doorstep of a house, was considered to be a way of preventing all members of the family living there from succumbing to sickness and ill health.

Edward Topsel, the English naturalist, writing in 1658 stipulated that, to cure blindness, or pains in the eye: 'Take the head of a black Cat, *which hath not a spot of another colour in it*, and burn it to powder in an earthen pot leaded or glazed within, then take this powder and through a quill blow it thrice a day into the eye' – the italics were not used in the original, but are to draw attention to the crucial quality of the black cat who is about to lose his head. So, after many years of religious selection pressure working against the pure-black cat, there was now the added pressure of medical quackery. Little wonder that today's black moggies so frequently sprout a small patch of white hairs as a badge of protection from earlier human follies.

Today a pure-black cat is probably a special pedigree specimen. Since competitive cat shows began, there has been a third selection pressure operating on feline coat colours – that of purification. Now, any kitten with tufts or streaks of white hair on an otherwise jet black coat will be ignored. Only those without such adornments – once so vital – will be selected for further breeding. Even so, it is significant that in most of the volumes on cat breeding and pedigree standards, there is a small, tell-tale phrase under the heading of 'coat colours', which states that the fur 'should be dense with no trace of white hairs'. The need to make such a comment for a pedigree breed that is clearly stated to be all-black in colour is a powerful reminder that the little white patches and flashes are still persisting, even after a century of specialized, selective breeding.

For those of us with non-pedigree black moggies which sprout a few white hairs, it is comforting to think of their special markings not as some kind of mongrel flaw but instead as a vital and valuable relic of earlier days in the feline history of Europe.

How does temperature affect the colour of a cat's fur?

When we look at the colour pattern of a cat we automatically think of it as something the animal inherits from its parents. In our minds it is a fixed pattern that is uninfluenced by variations in the animal's personal environment. It is a case of 'born a black cat, always a black cat', or 'born a sealpoint, always a sealpoint'. So it comes as a surprise to discover that this is not always the case. In one major group of cats – the Siamese – the colouring of the animals depends on the temperature in which they live.

When a Siamese kitten is born its fur is all-white. As it grows, this plain colouring begins to change. Dark pigments appear at the tip of the nose, around the edges of the ears, at the very tip of the tail and on the pads of the feet. These dark-ening extremities, or 'points', then slowly spread as the young cat becomes mature and by the end of the first year the Siamese has its adult pattern, with the nose colour covering most of its face, the dark ear-fringe spreading to include most of its ear surface, the tail-tip colour extending right up to near the base of its tail, and the pigment at the feet stretching halfway up its legs. At the places where the dark zones meet the pale central part of the body there is a soft intermediate zone, rather than a sharp edge.

This coloration is extremely attractive to human eyes and most people think of it as just another feline coat pattern, like tabby or tortoiseshell, but it arises in a completely different way. This is shown by looking at what happens when a Siamese kitten is reared in a very cold environment. Such an animal, born white as usual, darkens dramatically as it grows older. Instead of having a pale body with dark points, it becomes dark all over. Another Siamese kitten, reared in an unusually hot environment, develops an adult coat that is pale all over, lacking the dark points altogether.

The explanation of these variations is that, in the Siamese

cat, a lower skin temperature causes more pigmentation to be laid down in the growing hairs. This is why the newborn kitten, hot from its mother's womb, is white all over. Then, as it grows up in a normal, average temperature, the hotter area of its body – its central trunk region – remains pale in colour, while its cooler extremities become gradually darker. There is just enough difference between, say, the tip of the tail and the soft flanks of the cat, to produce the typical two-tone pattern of the Siamese. In fact, to study the sealpoint Siamese coat pattern is to observe what amounts to a temperature map of the animal's body surface.

Interestingly, if a Siamese cat is injured on one leg or its tail, and the damaged part is bandaged up while it recovers, this will have an impact on its coat colour. The hairs that start growing under the bandage – where the encased skin is hotter than usual – will lack pigmentation. When the bandage is removed there will at first be no sign of this. The old, dark hairs do not, of course, change. But later on, when the hairs that began sprouting in the heat of the bandage become fully grown and replace the old hairs, a startling white patch will appear. For pet cats this can be strangely disfiguring, upsetting the neat balance of the Siamese sealpoint pattern, and for pedigree show cats it can be disastrous, robbing them of any chance of winning a competition, at least until another whole growth of hairs has occurred and the white ones replaced in their turn.

Sometimes a Siamese cat will develop pale colouring on its points without any local injury. When this happens it means that the animal has suffered some kind of temperature-increasing illness, such as a prolonged fever, or possibly some kind of shock or trauma. For these reasons, the Siamese has to be kept calm and healthy if it is to retain its beautiful sealpoint pattern. Even with healthy Siamese, however, there is a problem for the pedigree exhibition cat, because as an animal grows older its general body temperature begins to fall very slightly, causing its body fur to darken little by little. As a result, a champion Siamese cat's career is usually over after only three or four years, as the hot-blooded youngster matures gracefully into the cool cat of older years.

When was the cat first domesticated?

In most cat books, the figure given for the first domestication of the cat is between 3,500 and 4,500 years ago. This is because we have fairly strong evidence from ancient Egyptian art, showing that cats had been taken under human control by that period. It is suggested that it was the great grain stores of the early Egyptian civilization that attracted the local wild cats. The stores were overrun with rats and mice and the cats came to feast on these rodent pests, thereby endearing themselves to the Egyptian people. But there is now some new evidence that means we will have to reconsider this picture of man's first close bond with the cat.

The Egyptian connection undoubtedly occurred, but it looks as though it was quite a late development. Several thousand years earlier, man and cat appear to have already developed a special relationship, and we can now state with reasonable certainty that the cat was domesticated at least eight thousand years ago.

The evidence is slender – nothing more than a feline jaw-bone – but it is convincing for a special reason. It was discovered as recently as 1983 by Alain le Brun when excavating at the Neolithic settlement of Khirokitia in southern Cyprus and has been found to date from 6000 B.C. The important point about its location is that Cyprus has no wild cats and this means that the animal must have been brought over to the island by the early human settlers. We know that they brought other domestic animals with them but it is inconceivable that they would have taken a wild cat from the mainland. A spitting, scratching, panic-stricken wild feline would have been the last kind of boat-companion they would have wanted. Only tame, domesticated animals could possibly have been part of the goods and chattels of that early band of pioneers, striking out for a new island home.

It seems almost certain, therefore, that cats had already been tamed and domesticated on the nearby mainland by 6000 B.C., and we should not be too surprised by this. Mankind had, after all, turned from hunting to farming as a way of life at least a thousand years before this date, by which time both goats and sheep were already domesticated. Crops were already being grown and were undoubtedly attracting rats and mice in large numbers. So the cat was badly needed even at this early date. Indeed, cat bones have been found associated with human settlements such as Jericho as early as nine thousand years ago, but in those cases – until now – we could not be certain about their significance. There were plenty of wild cats living in the nearby countryside and the inhabitants of Jericho may simply have trapped or hunted these wild felines and then eaten them. The bones provided no proof of taming or domestication. But this new bone is much stronger evidence. What is more, careful examination of its proportions has revealed that it belonged to precisely the same species of cat that was later domesticated in Egypt. So the cat is, after all, not one of our more recent animal companions, but one of our oldest. And, who knows, perhaps one day in the future we will find further evidence from an even earlier date, to take the domestic cat right back to the very beginning of the Neolithic period, some ten thousand years ago.

What is the history of the tabby cat?

The tabby cat is the most common colour form of all domestic breeds. It has a strange history and to understand it it is necessary to turn the clock back eight thousand years, to the moment when the first cats were being domesticated in the Middle East.

The cat from which our domesticated animals originated was the African wild cat. Despite its name, it is found over a very wide range of warm countries, including not only most of Africa but also the Mediterranean islands of Majorca, Corsica, Sardinia, Sicily and Crete. It also spreads right through Arabia and the Middle East as far as India and Turkestan. Farther north it is replaced by the European wild cat, which ranges from Portugal and Britain in the west to Russia in the east. Together they make up the species called *Felis sylvestris*.

The differences between these two races of wild cat support the idea that it was the African that originally gave rise to the domesticated feline. The European is too sturdy, with a broad head and a short, bushy tail that has a blunt, rounded tip. It is extremely difficult to tame and its shyness, combined with its great ferocity when cornered, suggests that it would have been troublesome for early man to domesticate.

The African wild cat, although bigger than the modern domestic cat, has a much less stocky body than the European wild cat, with an overall shape that is much closer to that of our familiar pet cats. Its head is more delicate and its tail less bushy. Above all, it is far less retiring than the European race and often approaches human settlements in search of the rodents that are plentiful there. One Victorian explorer reported that he could catch these cats and tether them near his food stores to keep the rats down. He claimed that they soon adapted to life in captivity and became useful pest-controllers. If young kittens were caught by local people they were said to become tame very quickly. This is a stark contrast to the spitting fury of the European wild cat. It is easy to imagine how

94

the early inhabitants of the Middle East, and in particular the ancient Egyptians, could have converted this African race into a domestic partner and there is little doubt that this is what occurred, with the more northerly European form being left out of the story altogether in the initial stages.

The coat pattern of both the European and the African races can best be described as suppressed, weak or washed-out tabby. The pattern is there but it is not impressive. This is undoubtedly what the original domestic cats looked like and wall paintings confirm that three to four thousand years ago the Egyptian cats had light or broken stripes. So how did the full-blooded tabby pattern arise?

The answer appears to be that it arrived courtesy of the Romans. The ancient Egyptians had been trying for centuries to prevent the export of their sacred felines. But Phoenician traders were notorious for their shady dealings around the Mediterranean and if there was a precious commodity for which they could find a ready market, nothing could stop them. Cats soon found their way out of Egypt, smuggled carefully to Greece and later to Rome. From there, they spread across Europe as the Roman empire began to swell. Along the way, these early pest-controlling cats started to encounter the wild European cats and to hybridize with them. The result of this injection of European blood was the original full-tabby cat. Tests have since shown that when the weak-tabby European and African wild cats are crossed with one another, the hybrid kittens develop coat patterns which are much closer to the tabby patterns of modern domestic cats than they are to the markings of either of their parents. This, it seems, is how the history of the tabby began.

The first cats of this type were what we today call striped or mackerel tabby, covered with thin, dark lines. Some of these lines break up into dashes or spots, but the overall effect is of a tigerish striping. To begin with, this was the only such pattern in existence, but then a new mutation arose. A blotched tabby appeared on the scene. On this animal the markings were much bolder and more complex. The narrow striping survived only in certain areas. It is believed that these blotched tabbies arose first in Britain, in the Elizabethan era. It was a time of great British expansion and it is thought that, in the guise of ships' cats, they were scattered from the British Isles all over the globe in a comparatively short space of time. With the growth of the British Empire in Victorian times, they spread still farther.

For some reason we do not fully understand, the blotched tabby cat was a winner. Perhaps the gene for the pattern was linked to an unusual level of aggressiveness or assertiveness, with the result that these cats soon managed to oust most other colour forms whenever there was a dispute over territory or females. Perhaps they were simply more healthy or more fertile. Whatever the reason, this new pattern began to dominate. The earlier striped tabby went into a rapid decline. Today it has become quite rare, while the blotched tabby is the most common colour form of all.

It would not be too far from the truth, as one author put it, to christen this most successful of all cats as 'The British Imperial Cat'.

How did the Manx cat lose its tail?

The tailless Manx cat is one of the oldest breeds known, having appeared on the Isle of Man at least four hundred years ago. In legend, it lost its tail because it was the last animal to board the ark. With the great flood rising fast, Noah slammed the door of the ark shut in such a hurry that he accidentally severed the cat's fine bushy tail.

In reality, the tailless condition is a genetic deformity of a rather serious kind. The gene that causes the taillessness also distorts the rest of the spine, giving the cat a backbone with fewer and shorter vertebrae. In severe cases it gives rise to the condition known as spina bifida. It also gives the animal unusually short front legs and long hind legs, and an abnormally small anus, so that it hops along like a rabbit and suffers from constipation.

There is also a lethal factor in the Manx gene. If two tailless Manx cats are mated, the kittens are so deformed that they nearly always die before birth. So Manx kittens are usually produced by crossing tailless cats with tailed ones. This gives rise to litters in which there are some *rumpies* (with no tails at all), some *rumpy-risers* (with a knob of a tail), some *stumpies* or *stubbies* (with very short tails) and some *longies* (with almost full-length tails).

How the Manx cat first arrived on the Isle of Man is hotly debated. One favourite story is that they were brought there from Japan by Phoenician traders thousands of years ago. This is based on the existence of a nearly tailless cat found in Japan – the Japanese Bobtail. Unfortunately for this theory, the genes carrying tail-reduction in the two cases are quite different, and the Manx and the Bobtail bear only a superficial resemblance to one another.

A second scenario pictures the original Manx cat swimming gamely ashore from one of the Spanish ships of the Armada escaping from the English fleet in 1588. The captain of this ship, we are told, ran his vessel aground on what is now known as The Spanish Rock and one or more tailless cats clambered to safety there. These cats were supposed to have been obtained by the Spanish captain from some unspecified source in the Middle East. A less glamorous version of its origin sees the first Manx cat as nothing more than a Manx sailor's pet – a curiosity brought home after travels to the Orient.

While everyone puzzles over how these animals first arrived on the Isle of Man, stories of tailless cats being found in such faraway places as Russia, Malaysia, and China all leading to new theories, nobody seems to have considered that the tailless gene might first have occurred on the Isle of Man itself. As a sudden mutation there is no reason whatever why it should not crop up anywhere, and the small island between Ireland and England is as likely a place for it as anywhere else.

Which are the giants and midgets of the cat world?

The size of domestic cats varies far less than that of domestic dogs. Dogs have been bred for many different tasks, from the massive guard dogs and fighting dogs right down to the little toy dogs and lap-dogs. But the cat has only had one main task throughout its long history of domestication and that is vermin-killing. This occupation has had little influence on its size. The North African wild cat weighs only slightly more than the average moggie.

So the giants and the midgets of the cat world are not particularly impressive. They do exist, however, because certain breeds of cat have become adapted to different climates. As with all animals, the colder the climate the bigger the body becomes. Modern breeds derived from northern European cats should therefore be heavier than those from the tropics. This is indeed what we find. The British Shorthair, descended from generations of felines that struggled to survive in the bleak climate of their island home, is stocky and sturdy and much more massive in build than, say, the lean-bodied Siamese from the steamy heat of Bangkok. Fully-grown tom-cats of these two contrasting breeds would weigh approximately 12 lbs and 9 lbs respectively.

A typical moggie is intermediate between these two extremes, with a tom weighing in at about 10 lbs and a queen at 8 lbs. A few freaks have been discovered from time to time, one amazing animal tipping the scales at no less than 43 lbs and a dwarf specimen at as little as 3 lbs, but these were abnormal. The giant was suffering from hormonal imbalance and the midget was a case of genetic dwarfism.

Among the pedigree breeds, the Maine Coon cat from North America is one of the biggest, with some exceptional individuals weighing as much as 30 lbs. The Norwegian Forest cat is another large breed, coming as it does from the coldest part of the domestic cat's range.

The smallest breed is one that has only recently arrived from Singapore, where it was known as the 'drain cat'. Cats are not particularly popular there, it seems, and this particular breed became smaller and smaller as an adaptation not only to the hot climates but also to the need to find restricted hiding-places. It was not officially 'discovered' until the 1970s, when a few were brought to the United States. There it is becoming increasingly popular, presumably because its diminutive body suits the increasing shift towards apartment-dwelling among modern Americans. Male Singapuras weigh, on average, only 6 lbs, and the females a mere 4 lbs.

Are some breeds abnormal?

There is a great deal of argument about what constitutes an abnormality in the world of pedigree cats. A new colour form creates no problems, but when a mutation occurs that alters the anatomy of the cat in some way, there is often a heated debate as to whether the new variant should be encouraged or allowed to die out. If it puts the cat at a major disadvantage then the answer is obvious, but if it is only a minor disadvantage then the cat breeders split into two warring camps. The result is that one official feline organization will recognize the new mutation as an additional breed, while another official body outlaws it and refuses to allow it to enter its cat shows.

At the present time there are four unusual breeds that fall into this category – accepted by some, rejected by others – and they are the Scottish Fold cat, the Canadian Sphynx cat, the Californian Ragdoll cat and the American Peke-faced cat. The Peke-faced cat was known back in the 1930s, but the other three were all discovered in the 1960s and were quickly established by enthusiastic local breeders, delighted to be founding new lines of pedigree cats. As there are fewer than fifty major breeds (ignoring all the colour variants), the discovery of entirely new types was extremely exciting, and the intense interest aroused by them is easy to understand. But, in the euphoria of the moment, were the local breeders blinding themselves to the fact that what they were really doing was preserving freaks? The only way to decide is to assess the situation in each case in terms of the cat's quality of life.

First, the Scottish Fold. There are many breeds of flop-eared dogs, but this is the only breed of cat that lacks the typical, pricked ears of the feline head. Its name refers to the fact that its ears are folded forwards so that, from the front, they appear to be horizontal in general shape, rather than vertical. The Fold cat was first spotted by a Scottish shepherd on a farm in 1961. He immediately realized that this was a most unusual kind of cat and started a breeding programme. The round-headed silhouette of the Scottish Fold gained it many admirers, although some felt it looked too sad. It was later discovered that some Scottish Folds developed thickening of the limbs and tail, and that this was a serious handicap to them. Such specimens have not been bred from since their problem was discovered, and the breed is now well established with no apparent weaknesses. It has become extremely popular in the United States, but certain official bodies are still banning it because, they say, the cat might suffer from ear mites or from deafness. The breeders of Scottish Folds retort that there is no evidence for this, and there the matter rests.

From the cat's point of view, the folded ears have the slight disadvantage that they do not communicate the usual mood signals seen when a cat, becoming angry or scared, starts to flatten its ears ready for fighting. It is the shift from fully erect ears to fully flattened ones that transmits the all-important social signal. The Scottish Fold cat appears as though it is permanently in the act of lowering its ears. This should make it look like a cat about to fight, but strangely it does not. The reason is that the folding of the ears brings them forward and this places them in a posture that is not part of the usual ear-lowering signal. In a normal cat, ears flattened to this degree would already be twisted round to the rear. So the Scottish Fold has a unique, 'squashed' ear, as distinct from a 'flattened' ear posture. Whether the cats themselves make this distinction no one seems to know. If they do, then there is no reason why this breed should not take its place among the other pedigree types.

Second, the Canadian Sphynx. This is a naked cat which was first discovered in Ontario in 1966. Apart from the fact that it lacks a coat of fur, it is a perfectly normal cat, with a charming disposition. But its nakedness does make it appear extremely ugly to many cat enthusiasts and does not seem to compensate for its oddity-value. The only serious objection to it is that it must suffer badly from the cold and, in its country of origin at least, it must spend the whole of the winter either indoors or in a man-made coat. If it has loving owners who can afford central heating, this breed presents no problems, but it has remained largely outlawed by the various cat societies.

Third, the Californian Ragdoll. This is a cat with a limp

body that genetically lacks the usual defensive reactions of felines. If picked up it hangs limply in your hands like a lifeless ragdoll and never tries to struggle. The fear for it is that it could easily be hurt without complaining and could suffer at the hands of careless children who would treat it too much like its namesake. What saves an ordinary cat from being over-mauled is the fact that sooner or later it struggles and scratches. But the Ragdoll, lacking these responses, could be literally loved to death by unthinking children. As a result, it too is banned by many cat societies, who would like to see it disappear altogether. The pity of it is that this happens to be as beautiful a cat as the Sphynx is ugly. Its defenders say that they will always keep its price high and carefully screen potential owners, as a way of protecting it. But how long could they keep control of the situation? This remains to be resolved.

Finally, the American Peke-faced cat is a long-haired breed that has been bred for a flatter and flatter face, rather as the Pekinese has been exaggerated among the dog breeds. As a result it suffers from problems with its eyes, its teeth and its breathing. Because of constriction beneath its eyes, its tear ducts can become blocked, causing runny eyes. Because of its reduced jaws, its teeth often fail to meet properly when the mouth is closed. And because of its reduced nasal cavities it may find breathing increasingly difficult as it grows older. Despite this, it does have an immensely attractive head-shape when viewed anthropomorphically. Its flattened face and its long, soft fur give it the rounded appearance of a 'super-baby', appealing to many humans. Because of this it has been popular at cat shows in the United States for several decades. But it still remains to be accepted in Britain as a suitable pedigree cat for championship status.

These four 'abnormal' breeds are all comparatively new, so they still have an uphill struggle to gain worldwide recognition. The long-established Manx cat is certainly as abnormal as any of them, with its strangely abbreviated backbone and the problems this causes, but its presence at cat shows was accepted so long ago that nobody now objects to its inclusion. And there would be a great sadness if it vanished, because it has become part of feline history.

Of the four new breeds, three are in no trouble providing

they are well looked after. If the Scottish Fold has its ears cleaned, the Canadian Sphynx is kept warm and the Californian Ragdoll is kept away from juvenile tormentors, they can all lead contented and fulfilled lives. The Peke-faced cat is another question. No matter how much love and attention this animal has, there is a danger that its respiration will suffer. So, for the sake of the animals themselves, this breed should be brought back slightly from its extremes of exaggeration. It will still be possible to have a charmingly flattened face, which transmits all those appealing baby-signals, even if not quite *so* flat. Moderation in all things has generally been a vain hope where human competition is concerned, and the contest to obtain the ultimate Peke-faced specimen has already led the breed into trouble. But the authorities of the cat world do seem to have their eyes firmly fixed on possible dangers, and we can hope for a much greater restraint than has existed in the case of a number of breeds of dog.

Why do so many cat breeds come from the East?

If you visit a major cat show today you will find that there are about fifty breeds on display there, in addition to the many different colour forms and 'sub-breeds', all minor variations of well-established breeds, which need not concern us here.

A survey of the country of origin of each breed reveals a strange distribution. Although Europe is the original home of the cat show and of competitive, controlled breeding, remarkably few of the fifty basic breeds come from that part of the world. Most of the old breeds come instead from the East. Before asking why, here is a summary of the facts:

Europe boasts the British Shorthair and its French counterpart, the Chartreux; also the large Norwegian Forest cat and, from the Isle of Man, the famous tailless Manx cat. Very recently, in the 1950s and 1960s, there have been the Rex cats and the Scottish Fold cat, and even more recently the Somali and the Burmilla, although these are little more than crosses. And that is about it.

The East, on the other hand, has given us the long-haired Persian cat from sixteenth-century Iran, the silky Angora cat from Turkey at the same period (when Ankara was pronounced Angora), and the exotic, long-legged Siamese cat from seventeenth-century Thailand. Other Oriental breeds include the Birman and the Burmese from Burma, the Turkish Van cat, the Japanese Bobtail, the Egyptian Mau cat, the Abyssinian cat from what is now Ethiopia, the Russian Blue, the Singapura from Singapore, and the Korat from Thailand.

Ignoring the very recent breeds, it is clear that in earlier days, when cat-showing was just beginning, the major pedigree lines nearly all stemmed from the Near or Far East, with the West lagging far behind. The reason for this is that, in Europe, the long centuries of persecution by the Christian Church had left the Western cat with a very low status. At worst it was looked upon as evil and at best no more than a utilitarian pest-destroyer. Only when we reach Victorian times do we find its status rising again, thanks to the sentimentality of the period. The climax of this change of mood was the holding of the first competitive cat show, at Crystal Palace in London in 1871. There were twenty-five classes and the animals were divided roughly into 'Eastern' and 'British'. As the years passed, the exotic Eastern cats gradually ousted the less exciting British cats and became the hot favourites, much to the distress of the British organizers.

The prominence of the Eastern cats was due to their more sacred and revered role in society. They had escaped the witch-hunt purges of Europe and had an entirely different significance in the lives of the Eastern peoples. Under the more favourable conditions of their past, they had developed into the remarkably beautiful and striking breeds that made such an impact on the visitors to the early cat shows. Even the very best British tabby had a difficult time competing with such dramatic animals.

If Europe had not suffered so many years of religious cruelty and persecution, the home-grown cats might have been better developed and ready to compete with the extravagant foreigners. But so few local breeds had undergone any kind of specialized breeding to improve the stock, and the Western animals had to attempt to catch up with their long-established and highly pampered Oriental counterparts.

Switching to modern times, the source of new breeds has moved to the North American continent. Cats developed in the United States and Canada include: the Peke-faced cat, the Ragdoll cat, the Balinese, the Maine Coon, the American Shorthair, the Snowshoe, the Havana Brown, the Ocicat, the Malayan, the Tonkinese, the Bombay, the Wirehair and the extraordinary Sphynx. Despite their often Eastern names, these are all Western pedigree cats, almost all of which have been specifically developed for the show-ring, rather than for any other purpose.

Africa, South America and Australia appear to have contributed little or nothing to the pedigree cat world. And Europe, with its disgraceful feline past, has provided far less than its fair share. In general, we have to thank the Orient for the early breeds and North America for the late ones.

How did the cat become associated with witchcraft?

Religious bigots have often employed the cunning device of converting other people's heroes into villains, to suit their own purposes. In this way, the ancient horned god that protected earlier cultures was first transformed into the evil Devil of Christianity. And the revered, sacred feline of ancient Egypt became the wicked, sorcerer's cat of medieval Europe. Anything considered holy by a previous religious faith must automatically be damned by a new religion. In this way began the darkest chapter in the cat's long association with mankind. For centuries it was persecuted and the cruelties heaped upon it were given the full backing of the Church.

During this bleak phase of its history the cat became firmly linked in the popular mind with witches and black magic. As late as 1658 Edward Topsel, in his serious work on natural history, followed detailed descriptions of the cat's anatomy and behaviour with the solemn comment that 'the familiars of Witches do most ordinarily appear in the shape of Cats, which is an argument that this beast is dangerous to soul and body.'

Because the cat was seen as evil, all kinds of frightening powers were attributed to it by the writers of the day. Its teeth were said to be venomous, its flesh poisonous, its hair lethal (causing suffocation if a few were accidentally swallowed), and its breath infectious, destroying human lungs and causing consumption. All this created something of a problem, since it was also recognized that cats were useful 'for the suppressing of small vermine'. Topsel's compromise was to suggest to his readers that 'with a wary and discreet eye we must avoid their harms, making more account of their use than of their persons'. In other words, exploit them, but do not get too close to them or show them any affection.

This restrained attitude did, at least, enable farm cats and some town cats to live a tolerable life as unloved pest-controllers, but for certain village cats life was far more unpleasant. If they happened to attach themselves to an old woman who lived by herself, they were risking a savage death as a witch's familiar. The sad irony of this unhappy state of affairs was that these animals played a comforting role in the lives of such old women. Any elderly crone, who happened to be ugly or misshapen enough to have repelled all potential husbands, and who was therefore forced to live a solitary life with no children of her own, often as an outcast on the edge of the village, was desperately in need of companionship. Maltreated cats, finding themselves in a similar plight, often approached such women, who befriended them as substitutes for human companionship and love. Together, they brought one another many rewards and the kindness of these old women towards their cats was excessive. Anyone teasing or hurting their beloved felines was cursed and threatened. All that was required then was for one of these tormentors to fall ill or suffer a sudden accident and the old 'witch' was to blame. Because the cats wandered about, often at night, they were thought to be either the supernatural servants of the witches, or else the witches themselves, transformed into cat-shape to aid their nocturnal travels when seeking revenge.

So it was the reaction against the cat's ancient 'holiness' in Egyptian religion, combined with its connection with childless, elderly women, that made it the 'wicked' animal of the medieval period. Added to this was its haughtiness and its refusal to become completely subservient to human demands, unlike the dog, the horse, the sheep and other easily controlled domestic animals. Also, its nocturnal caterwauling during the breeding season gave rise to tales of orgies and secret feline ceremonies. The outcome was a savage persecution lasting for several centuries, perpetrated against an animal whose only serious task was to rid human habitations of infestations of disease-carrying, food-spoiling rats and mice. It is a strange chapter in the history of Christian kindness.

Why does a black cat bring good luck?

In Britain it has long been believed that if a black cat crosses your path or enters your house it will bring you good fortune. This superstition has three origins.

The first source takes us back to ancient Egypt where the sacred cat was thought to bestow many blessings on the household that looked after it. Its real blessing, of course, was that it kept down the numbers of mice and rats. But this was extended, through myth and legend, to be seen as a generalized blessing. Ancient tomb inscriptions inform us that the cat 'gives life, prosperity and health every day, and long life and beautiful old age'. Clearly no home should be without one. By slender threads, this ancient tradition managed to cling on, century after century, even when the Christian Church started its onslaught against cats as the servants of the Devil.

The second source is from medieval times, when the 'devil-cat' was feared and hated. It was then believed that if a cat crossed your path and did you no harm, you had been incredibly lucky. Hence the association between cats and good luck. If one came into your house then, by being kind to it, you could appease its master, the Devil, and avoid his wrath. So a cat entering your house and being welcomed there gave you the good luck of having the Devil on your side. Others might be tormented by him, but not you.

The third source is more down to earth. An old British saying is: 'Whenever the cat of the house is black, the lasses of lovers will have no lack.' Here the cat is being used as a symbol of sexual attraction. The female cat on heat attracts a whole circle of admiring tom-cats, and the house with such a cat is therefore a place where perhaps any female, even human, would be successful at attracting a large circle of male admirers.

The colour black in all such cases was considered especially lucky because this was the colour associated with the occult practices, but herein lies a transatlantic contradiction for, in

America, it is the white cat that is lucky and the black cat that is unlucky. There it seems that from the earliest days of the pioneer settlers the black cat was linked with the devil so strongly that it was, in any context, an evil force. Nobody was prepared to have any dealings with this force, even to attempt to pacify it by being kind to the black cat. The white cat, presumably by direct contrast, was seen as a force of light against the darkness and was in this way converted into a symbol of good fortune.

How has the cat been used in warfare?

Although it is common knowledge that dogs have been extensively employed in times of war, most people imagine that the cat has never been exploited in this way. But they are wrong. There are two examples, albeit somewhat unusual ones.

The first dates back two and a half thousand years to the time when the Persians were at war with the Egyptians. Knowing that the Egyptians revered the cat and considered it to be sacred, the Persians developed the idea of a 'feline armour'. When their advance guard was making a hazardous push to secure a new stronghold, the Persian warriors went forward carrying live cats in their arms. Seeing this, the Egyptian soldiers were unable to attack them in case they accidentally injured or killed one of these sacred animals. For them, such act of violence against one of their animal deities was unthinkable. Indeed, if any one of them had killed a cat, even in these special circumstances, he would have been put to death for it. So in this way the Persians were able to advance with ease and the Egyptians were helpless to retaliate.

Incidentally, despite these defeats in war, the Egyptians did not weaken in their worship of the cat. We know from the observations of Herodotus nearly a century later that they were still treating the animal with the utmost respect. He reported that if a house caught fire nobody attempted to put it out because they were all concentrating on protecting the cats, forming up in lines to prevent the panic-stricken animals from running into the flames and burning themselves. And whenever a cat died he noted that Egyptians all went into deep mourning and shaved off their eyebrows as a sign of their distress. So it is little wonder that the Persians found the cat an invaluable ally even at the height of battle.

The second example of the use of cats in warfare appears much later, being illustrated in Christopher of Hapsburg's book in the year 1535. He was an artillery officer and in his report to the Council of One and Twenty at Strasbourg he described the way in which 'poisoned vapours were shed abroad' by means of cats. The unfortunate animals apparently had poison bottles strapped to their backs, with the openings pointing towards their tails. They were then sent off towards the enemy, running panic-stricken this way and that, and in the process spreading the poisonous fumes. Christopher of Hapsburg was clearly a man of delicate sensibilities, for he adds the comment, 'This process ought not to be directed against Christians.'

Why do we say that someone is grinning like a Cheshire Cat?

In Lewis Carroll's *Alice in Wonderland* we encounter a large cat, lying on the hearth and grinning from ear to ear. Alice is told that the reason it is grinning is because it is a Cheshire Cat. There is, however, no explanation as to why cats from that particular English county should be prone to smiling. A clue comes with the final disappearance of the cat, when it slowly vanishes, starting with the end of its tail and ending with the broad grin, which remains some time after the rest of the animal has gone. It is this disembodied grin that explains the source of Lewis Carroll's image, for there used to be a special kind of Cheshire cheese which had a grinning feline face marked on one end of it. The rest of the cat was omitted by the cheesemaker, giving the impression that all but the grin had vanished.

Lewis Carroll may well have seen these cheeses. But he may have taken his reference from an even earlier source. The reason why the Cheshire cheesemakers saw fit to add a grinning cat to their product was because the expression to 'grin like a Cheshire Cat' was already in use for another reason altogether. It was an abbreviation of the saying to 'grin like a Cheshire Caterling', which was current about five centuries ago. Caterling was a lethal swordsman in the time of Richard III, a protector of the Royal Forests who was renowned for his evil grin, a grin that became even broader when he was despatching a poacher with his trusty sword. Caterling soon became shortened to 'Cat' and anyone adopting a particularly wicked smile was said to be 'grinning like a Cheshire Cat'. Lewis Carroll possibly knew of this phrase but, because he refers to the grin outlasting the rest of the body, it is more likely that his real influence was the cheese rather than the swordsman.

Whichever is the case, the fact remains that the saying does not start with Carroll, as most people assume, but was in reality much older and was merely borrowed and made more famous by him.

Why is a non-pedigree cat called a moggie?

A non-pedigree dog is always referred to as a mongrel and, strictly speaking, this is the correct term for a non-pedigree cat, but few people use it in this way. They are much more likely to call their pet feline a 'moggie' (sometimes spelt moggy).

Despite its popularity, few people seem to know the origin of the term. It began life as a local dialect variant of the name 'Maggie' and its original meaning was 'a dishevelled old woman'. In some regions it was also the name given to a scarecrow and the essence of its meaning was that something was scruffy and untidy. By the start of the present century its use had spread to include cats. This seems to have begun in London where there were countless scruffy alley-cats whose poor condition doubtless led to the comparison with 'dishevelled old women'.

By the inter-war period the word moggie had been abbreviated to 'mog' and in the 1920s and 1930s schoolboy slang referred to dogs and cats as 'tikes and mogs'. For some reason, this shortened form fell into disuse after the Second World War and the more affectionate 'moggie' returned as the popular term for the ordinary, common-or-garden cat.